The Cyclone Mom Method

How to Call Upon Your God-Given Power to Remain Calm, In Control, and Confident as a Busy Mom

Danielle Thienel

Table of Contents

Introduction

You have God-given, God-created power to experience a calm confidence in the midst of the storms of life. A cyclone is a kind of storm that draws its power from a calm center. Without a calm center, a cyclone can't move forward. It can't even carry out what it was created by God to be. Moms work the same way.

That's why I chose a cyclone as the metaphor for my method. I want you to tap into a God-given power to be a calm mom, an in-control mom, and a confident mom. I want you to become a Cyclone Mom.

When the difficulties of life swirl around you, it is possible to stand grounded, firm, and steadfast as you live the life you've always wanted.

This outcome is what drew me to life coaching in the first place. First, for my own sake, and later, for the sake of every mother I can contact and influence.

I know what it feels like to be overwhelmed, to be so hopelessly drowning in your own life that you feel like you can't ever catch up, and to feel as if it's your own fault you feel so powerless. You might know it's possible to experience joy and balance, but you believe it's just not in the cards for you.

I wrote this book thinking of a mom who believes all of these things about herself. I imagined her sitting on the closet floor just trying to catch her breath, maybe crying, most likely grabbing a sweet treat to snack on as she tries to carve out just a few minutes for herself in a desperate quest to enjoy a moment of respite as she navigates her current stage of motherhood.

I am here to help you.

This book is structured in a specific way and is likely different from any other book on motherhood you've read before.

To begin, we'll identify and explore the challenges mamas face. You're familiar with these, but don't skip over them. There are insights you need in these chapters.

I'll then teach you the number one key that unlocks it all and that begins the almighty shift from where you are now to where you can be.

I include some education about your brain and your body that I wish were taught in common spaces in our society but are not. I want you to know that there's nothing broken about you. There's nothing missing that others have and you don't have. I want to include this knowledge for you for two reasons:

1) It's not your fault, and you likely believe it is. This overwhelming feeling that keeps you up at night, this despair that things might never improve, and this inability you feel that you have to accomplish your dreams - there's actually a simple principle behind it all that I didn't learn until I was well into my motherhood journey that I want to teach you here.

2) Understanding this principle helps you step into the aforementioned God-given power. This knowledge will change how you approach your day-to-day life for the better.

After this revelation, I give you everything I have, from the five steps of my Cyclone Mom Method to a few of my favorite tools to help you get started and follow through on these changes you so desperately want to see in your life.

Now, let me be upfront. I want to coach you. I want to be your coach. I want to help you personally. If you're in a position for that, there are places throughout this book where I prompt you to reach out and get in touch with me.

But, even if personal life coaching is not in the cards for you right now, this book is designed to get you started. It's designed to accomplish some of the major shifts I've seen my mom clients need in their early coaching days.

Please read this with an open mind and an open heart.

The very first step of my Cyclone Mom Method is to call on your faith in your life. I want you to know that I have done this as I have written this book. I have prayed over what content to include, what words of encouragement to say, and what lessons will carry you the furthest.

I prayed for you, wonderful mama, and this book is the gift I felt I could give to you.

In the name of the Father, and of the Son, and of the Holy Spirit, let's get started. I can't wait to show you the way.

Danielle

PART 1:

THE CYCLONE SWIRL

CHAPTER 1:

Your Power in the Storm

You will keep those in perfect peace, whose mind is stayed on You. ~Isaiah 26:3

How are you feeling today?

Honestly. You're not responding to a post on social media here. You can be honest.

Are you happy? Overwhelmed? Busy? Anxious?

I ask because this is where everything starts. Everyone can identify whether they are feeling good or feeling bad.

My number one goal is to help you, mama, to feel better than you do at this exact moment.

At one point in my life, I remember feeling overwhelmed and out of balance with all of the tasks around me. I had three, school-aged children, I had a job outside of my home, and I was coordinating the build of a nearby home for my parents to move into.

I'll skip over the more unpleasant parts of that story for now. Suffice it to say that I was burned out and ready to quit. As if on cue, my body gave up. I got sick, sicker than I've ever been before, and that caused me to pause and reflect.

I started implementing some of the methods I will teach you within the pages of this book, and suddenly, I started having thoughts like, "I have plenty of time today. While the kids are getting off to school, I get to do what I want to do. What sounds exciting to me to do?"

I started spending an hour with Christ in the mornings. That felt amazing. I was able to run to Michael's and help my daughter with a project she needed supplies for without it being an extra strain on my schedule. My husband needed dry cleaning picked up. Sure. No problem. I got it.

I felt at ease and in control with very little actually changing around me.

I can almost hear the rebuttal as I write this. "But Danielle, I can't quit my job. I can't leave my life. There's nothing I can do to change my current circumstances. I'm stuck, I feel hopeless, and I don't think anything will work for me."

I know. The storm doesn't stop raging. It might sit dormant for a season, but life's difficulties don't stop coming for us.

This is why I chose a cyclone as my metaphor for this method I teach my clients.

But first, I want to point out a couple of aspects from my personal story.

The circumstances didn't entirely change. My thoughts were what changed first. My feelings followed, and the results cascaded their way through my life. I'll speak more about this in depth later, but I want to plant this seed now: your circumstances do not create your feelings. Circumstances are not why you feel good, bad, positive, or negative.

The wind, the storm, the swirl that threaten to toss you to and fro - there is a way to experience these things and feel calm, in control, and confident.

As I wrote earlier, a cyclone is the perfect representation of life because when I picture it, it never stops. It never goes away. Different circumstances may come and go, but there will always be situations, things, and experiences that are happening around us and to us. Always. That is our earthly experience. There will always be something that swirls around us.

That swirl can be anything. Having kids. Somebody dying. Starting a job. Stopping a job. Having to clean the house. Pining for your own home to clean. Having to maintain your weight or build up your savings account. Having a big bill come into your life you weren't expecting. An actual storm that knocks down your house.

So, knowing the swirl will always be there around you, my question is this: what do you want to do about it?

Do you want to always be in the swirl, feeling stressed and overwhelmed? Or, do you want to learn how to feel in control no matter what life throws your way or what happens around you?

Sure. You'll have times where things are great and you don't feel chaotic. You're going to soak that up, as you should.

But, with my method, you're not going to be knocked off balance when the swirl picks up speed. What I'm teaching you in the pages of this book is so much more than affirmations and checklists. It's a completely new way of thinking.

My goal for you is that when you transition from a time of peace into another cyclone, you'll say, "That's normal," because you *have the control to feel any way you want no matter what life brings you.* No matter what circumstance you're in, you have the power to choose your feelings.

I know that sounds impossible right now.

From the moms I have worked with, I know you want to feel in control. You've tried everything you can, and nothing has worked. I know how awful it feels to be out of control in spite of your best, most heartfelt efforts. I know what it feels like to be knocked down when your flood of thoughts is, "No, no, no. That wasn't supposed to happen! I don't want this! Take it back!"

I'm here to tell you that you can take control, even if you can't change your circumstances.

When the swirl is happening around you, there is a way to feel calm and balanced instead of stressed and overwhelmed. I am here to teach you and guide you through this process.

When a storm rages, you'll find you have a whole new power that you didn't know you had before because it's within your own brain.

Prior to this, you were at the mercy of what was happening around you: other people's actions, unpredictable events, the weather.

After this book, you will feel however you want no matter what else is happening. You will take action in your life because you have the right feelings to drive those actions.

I'm not the only one who feels empowered and centered on a daily basis. Here are a few words from past and current clients.

> ### Jessica Goes from Survival Mode to Balanced
>
> *Before I started coaching, I felt stuck, like I was underperforming and falling short in so many aspects of my life. I didn't believe there was any way I could balance it all. I was afraid to try one more thing and fail, but I knew I wanted to see change in my life. Committing to coaching was the best investment I could have made in myself. **I felt safe, encouraged, and supported throughout the whole process, even when I was most vulnerable.** I initially wanted help figuring out how to lose weight and how to clear the clutter and keep a cleaner home. **I didn't expect to feel such a comprehensive, all-encompassing sense of change in my life, but literally every aspect of my day is impacted positively by the work we've done.** Coaching with Danielle has truly taken me from surviving to thriving, and I will forever be grateful for this opportunity to work on myself and soak up this profound knowledge.*

Maggie Breaks Out of a Rut and Confidently Pursues God's Plan

Reaching out to Danielle changed the trajectory of my future. Before working with her, I felt stuck in a rut and like I could never actually pursue the deepest desires of my heart. Well, she turned that lie on its head and revealed to me time and time again the truths I needed to embrace to stop getting in my own way. She was on point every time. Since working with her,

my marriage is stronger, my approach to motherhood is more peaceful, and my dreams are no longer being placed on hold. It's crazy to think I now have my own business at this stage of my life! **I am full of confidence, gratitude, and a heart that is finally trusting in God's plan for my life.** I am forever grateful for Danielle and the work she is doing to help women become fully alive.

Lorie Reframes Overwhelm and Chooses Peace and Confidence

Before I joined coaching, I was feeling very overwhelmed and stuck in my life. I had two very young children and felt like life was pulling me in all directions, and I had a hard time making decisions. I felt like I wasn't doing enough for myself, my kids, my husband, or my faith. During coaching, I learned that all of these feelings were because of my thoughts, and I learned tools to be able to manage these thoughts. Now, circumstances are the same (same kids, same house, same amount of time in the day, etc.), but **I feel much more peaceful about life. I learned that everything I do is a choice, and to own those choices is what brings me peace and confidence about my decisions.** Life is so much simpler and lighter. I don't have to be and do everything all the time. I also learned how to focus on my goals and achieve them. Danielle is awesome at what she does, and her passion for helping moms and her care for her clients shine through. Highly recommend!

Kristin Sheds Discouragement and Embraces Possibility

I was feeling disappointed, sad, discouraged, and even wondering if the goals I'd been working so hard at might not have been realistic after all. I was questioning everything. **Coaching showed me the ways my own thinking was causing me to feel so bad and how possible it truly was to achieve the goals I currently have** — and that I could even achieve bigger goals I have for the future. Danielle and coaching provided the relief I was seeking of having someone support me emotionally and mentally. Every week, she shows up for me with love, understanding, and a new perspective. I hadn't considered that my faith is of utmost importance to me. **I have loved having a coach who understands this devotion to God on a personal level and helps me see the links between the goals I'm trying to achieve and the worthiness and love I already have through Christ.**

> ### Racquel Builds Confidence and Grows in Motherhood and Business
>
> With Danielle's coaching on my side, I have been given back control over my brain. **I can create the life I've always dreamed of living** because she taught me how to let go of limiting beliefs that we all have the habit of letting circle around in our minds. I can't thank her enough for showing me how it is possible to bring joy into my life no matter the circumstance. It's funny how I've mainly pointed out how she's changed my life because I hired her to help me start up my business... which she did!!! **I confidently made decisions in my new business that led me to growing and making financial leaps that I would've never imagined possible** 3 months into a new business. There is so much more I hope to unpack with Danielle. I believe God has truly called her to do great things in the lives of her clients and listeners, and I'm so honored to be one of them!

> ### Kellie Takes Control and Becomes Who She's Always Wanted to Be
>
> Before coaching, I struggled with making my own decisions, enjoying the journey, recognizing my own boundaries, standing up for myself, and having the ability to dig deeper into my own mind. I realized I was giving my own peace and control away to others. I was not showing up as the person I wanted to be.
>
> Due to coaching, **I was able to navigate life circumstances all while showing up for myself and keeping peace in my life** - talk about a huge win while

raising three crazy boys! **I was able to recognize who I wanted to be, and I could easily change my thoughts in order to achieve the goals I desired and become the person I wanted to be.**

I am forever thankful for Danielle and for pouring her heart out to me, helping me to see the path to peace - and the greatest part is that it was already inside of me - I just had to tap into it!

More Empowered Moms

Working with Danielle has given me the right tools to get my new small business off to a great start. She has shown me the model to achieve my dreams by helping me to stay focused and put my priorities in perspective. She was very thoughtful, caring, and great to work with. Her enthusiasm has made it easy for me to open up to her about some issues that needed attention. I highly recommend Danielle to everyone!

~ Dawn

Having a life coach created a container where I felt seen and heard. Danielle's style is warm but direct, joyful, and "let's roll up our sleeves." - all important qualities in a coach. I experienced breakthroughs in my first session with her and left feeling energized. I highly recommend having her on your side!

~ Nicole

Life coaching helped me so much. I wasn't sure what I would get out of working with her, but now I feel an ease and lightness in place of the heaviness and overwhelm that I felt before. I'm feeling energized and clear in an area that I was previously feeling frustrated and stuck in.

~ Elizabeth

Life Coaching helped me recognize the hidden, negative thoughts holding me back from my goal! I can definitely see the limitation of trying to coach myself. Coaching was crucial to me because it allowed me to look deeper inside at what I am thinking and figure out how these thoughts are affecting my results! Danielle's support allowed me to recognize the truth about what I am thinking, and now I know the results I desire are within my reach.

~ Teresa

Coaching is a joint venture. While my clients so graciously thank me for my time and expertise, I always tell my mamas that you are the ones showing up and applying what you learn.

By picking up this book, you have said yes to yourself and to the voice inside of you that knows there's more to your experience here on Earth.

We are co-creating this new life with God. He gave us a brain that works in a specific way – a way that I have come to understand and teach to other moms so they can have peace, balance, and joy in their motherhood right now, whether they have little ones or an empty nest.

The power to feel this way is within you no matter what you face.

<table>
<tr><td>

Chapter 1 Key Takeaways

- The cyclone is the perfect representation of life because it's never-ending. There is always another circumstance or situation that arises, creating the swirl around us. Take a moment to imagine the swirl around you now. What are all your current circumstances that make up your swirl?

- You have the control to feel any way you want no matter what life brings you. List some ways you were able to feel in control before, even when it was a negative or tough experience that you weren't expecting.

- When the swirl of the cyclone surrounds you, there is a way to feel calm, confident, and in control (what this book is all about and will teach you).

- This framework I am going to give you here applies to moms of all situations and backgrounds. You are not so different that the principles in this book won't work for you.

- Keep going! I've got you covered.

</td></tr>
</table>

CHAPTER 2:

The Rhythm of a Busy Mom Life

Be Still and Know that I am God. ~Psalms 46:10

Go back with me to five years ago.

I knew nothing about life coaching. I had no Cyclone Mom Method.

I was a full-time mom to three kids: twin pre-teens and an elementary school aged child. They each had several activities going on: competitive gymnastics, dance, science extracurriculars, basketball, and soccer.

In the kid part of my world, I was driving and shuttling my kids from place to place.

As I mentioned before, I was also working part-time outside of our home.

My parents, who lived in my city, had an opportunity to move in across the street from us. We knew my parents were older in age, and we wanted them close to help take care of them, so we jumped at the opportunity. However, the process required conversations that had a bit of stress to them, plus we took it upon ourselves to renovate their new house to accommodate their needs.

This means I was also dealing with contractors on a weekly, if not daily, basis.

On top of all of this, I remember trying to do all of the normal life things: work out, maybe catch up with a friend, keep my marriage strong, and maintain a clean home to name a few.

I felt behind, not good enough, and stressed, like I was at the mercy of everything else in my life.

The contractor would come and tell me a part of the renovation was going to take twice as long and double the price. I was completely at their mercy with no power to change that.

My boss would ask me to do something, and I'd ask myself, "Is he serious, or is he just in a bad mood?" But, more than that, I knew this job wasn't something that fed my soul and was just a means to extra income.

My kids would come to me with their schedules and events that had them spread out across town but at the exact same time. I knew I'd miss one of them, and I didn't know how I could possibly show up as the mom I wanted to be in this situation.

I remember thinking that if my job wasn't draining me, if the kids would just be on time to get ready for their stuff, if the contractor was on time and it didn't cost as much, if my parents were happy about everything that was going on, and if my house was clean and organized, then - and only then - would I feel better.

I wouldn't be stressed out and mad. I wouldn't yell at the kids. I wouldn't feel tired and cranky all of the time. I wouldn't have any of these problems if everyone else would just get their act together.

I fell into the classic trap that so many of my clients do: "I'll feel better when…"

In the midst of the blame and the victimhood, I just kept thinking, "I'll figure it out. I'll get it done. I'm smart." I told myself, "Once it's summer break and the contractors are finished with the house, I'll feel better."

But then, I got sick with a full-body flu that then morphed into bronchitis. It was an agonizing two-week period where I was finally forced to be still.

There I was in bed, barely conscious. Just me and my thoughts. I started to reflect and reevaluate my life and realized that something had to change.

Especially because, contrary to what I had thought before, the world kept going on without me.

My kids got rides to their activities. My mom came in and helped with my house. The contractors continued their work without me checking in on them.

When I was honest with myself in relation to my job, I realized it did not fulfill me. It was draining, not soul-giving, and that needed to change. Quickly, a thought came, and I wanted the money I got from my job. "It's good for me to have something to strive for, and I do like helping people."

So, after my two-week illness, I found myself back at work, sitting at my computer, booting it up and preparing for another day. I was grateful for my health and my return to work.

The lock screen of my computer popped up with a serene picture of a beach (my happy place), prompting me to enter in my password. In that exact moment, the Holy Spirit spoke to me. I've had enough chances over the years to recognize it and paused, realizing this was something holy.

It said, "It's time to leave this job. It's time to be home. It's time to go home."

Of course, I sat there in my chair, dumbfounded, thinking, "Did I just hear that?"

You can probably guess the rest. I texted my husband, who had already told me that I didn't need to go back to a job I didn't love, and after giving notice, I left and went home.

The whole instance of getting sick and having the Holy Spirit move me helped me become the mom I really wanted to be. In the past, I thought it was what I needed to do. Help the kids. Help my parents. Work outside to get money for the family. Clean up the house - I thought that is what made me "the better mom."

But, all I did was become more exhausted and overwhelmed.

Through a series of events started from a nudge by my good friend, Connie, I started down the path of becoming a life coach (more on this later).

As a result of my changes and my study, I found my life was even better than I could have imagined:

- **I got clearer about what I wanted.** I started deciding what I actually liked and didn't like. I stopped concentrating on what I didn't want and what wasn't going well. My focus was on going after and achieving what I actually wanted, not what I thought society or other people would tell me to go after but what I felt like I, a good mom, should do.

- **I started making decisions and taking action.** I wanted to be the person who has an hour of prayer time in the morning. Instead of questioning it or parsing it down, I decided what time I would participate, what days I would pray, what books I wanted to have present, and so on. I clarified my goals so I knew where I was headed.

- **I felt happier and at peace**. My top three feelings had been overwhelm, guilt, and frustration. Now, they were in control, confident, and calm. My emotional life upleveled because I knew the source, my thoughts, determined my feelings. I felt empowered that I could feel any way I wanted at any given time.

- **I focused on progress and dropped perfectionism.** A tool I teach my clients is the concept of 'B-.' We'll get more into this later. I found that when I started focusing on getting things done, but not perfectly, I was able to get a pile of results. Things got done.

- **I felt closer to Christ.** I am more in the habit of pausing to ask myself, "What would God say to me right now?"

If I find myself rushing along, I remind myself that this is not God's rhythm. He is not found in the rush. When I'm about to do something scary, He says, "Don't be afraid. Take courage. You're going to learn from this."

- **I now know that nothing was wrong with me. I am not broken.** I don't ever have to answer the question, "Who am I to have this?" The fact that I exist, that I am created by God, and that He knows every count of hair on my head makes me never have to question my sense of worthiness again.

I could see the chains fall off, and I stepped out of a trap that was self-imposed.

These are the results my mamas experience with the Cyclone Mom Method because what I am really teaching you within the pages of this book is a new way to approach your whole life.

When I learned these methods, I felt a little duped because no one had ever taught me anything like it. If I had known then what I know now, I could have saved myself a lot of grief in the earlier stages of motherhood.

And that, saving yourself months or years of grief from living at the mercy of your circumstances, is what I am now here to help you do.

The number one thing you can do to move your life forward right now, at this moment, is to accept that negative feelings are a part of a healthy life. We'll talk about this more later on in this book, but I want to plant the concept. Everything you want in life requires some discomfort. There are times when anger, sadness, grief, etc., are an appropriate response to a given situation.

We are not here to avoid bad feelings. We are here to hold the reins and be in control of our lives and happiness.

It is my hope that by teaching you the Cyclone Mom Method, you will know how to call upon your God-given power to remain calm, in control, and confident through all the stages of your busy mom life.

If you are a mom who feels overwhelmed, burned out, not good enough, or like you are failing and falling behind, I am here to help you feel better. I am here to change how your life plays out, and by the end of this book, you'll have the tools and knowledge you need.

In the name of the Father, and of the Son, and of the Holy Spirit, let's get started.

Chapter 2 Key Takeaways

- In my journey, I felt overwhelmed, stressed, and at the mercy of everyone else around me. I couldn't be happy until someone else made a different choice. Where in your life do you delay joy because you are waiting for someone else to change?

- I felt a whisper from the Holy Spirit and followed it, but my journey had only begun! Can you take a few minutes right now or sometime today to purposely carve out at least 5 minutes for silence where you may feel a whisper too?

Chapter 2 Key Takeaways

- Though my life improved after this point, I realized I needed a bigger change. I learned from my life coaching how to get clear on my goals, make decisions and take action, be happy, drop perfectionism, and be closer to Christ. I learned that there was nothing wrong with me *just like there is nothing wrong with you.* Take a few moments now to picture how your life would be different if you no longer believed anything was wrong with you and instead decided what you wanted and knew it was possible for you to go get it.

- The top thing you can do to move your life forward is to accept that negative feelings are a part of a healthy life. Go google "feelings list" and see all the types of positive and negative feelings there are out there that make up this human experience for all of us.

CHAPTER 3:

Growing Pains

And the peace of God, which surpasses all understanding, will guard your hearts and minds in Christ Jesus. ~Philippians 4:7

In this chapter, I'd like to address the common pains and hurdles my mom clients face on a daily basis.

I know motherhood can be so tough. Every journey I have heard from my clients involves sacrifice and difficulty. The age-old saying that "it's the hardest and most rewarding job" seems to ring true for so many of the moms I work with. What's more, many of us accept things as our lot in life and we move forward, carrying a brick-laden backpack uphill without the right tools or help.

I'm here to change that by sharing the five most common obstacles my mamas face and a brief explanation of how we will tackle each one within this book.

Something is wrong with me. I feel ashamed. I'm a terrible mom.

It breaks my heart how many mothers come to me with the thought that there is something wrong with them.

"I must have a missing gene."

"I've tried, and nothing works."

"Other people do it so much better than me."

"I'll never figure this out."

When you are stuck in this belief system, it is impossible to live a life that God created for you. He did not create us to despair. He wants you to delight in the beauties of the Earth.

I remember once, before I was a coach, my neighbor came to me and confided that she had yelled at her daughter and said some very unkind words to her weeks prior to our conversation. She had been carrying guilt and shame about it around with her for weeks, feeling awful and isolated as the worst mom in the history of parenthood.

I replied that I experienced something similar within my motherhood journey. Something I had learned was, "It's okay. It happens. The best moms make mistakes."

You could see her shoulders visibly drop from the relief that she was not alone in her seeming failure.

This is the most common pain I see in the moms I work with. If you are feeling this way, you are not alone! This book was written for you.

Self-Assessment	
Instructions: Ask yourself each question, and indicate a 'Y' for yes or an 'N' for no.	
Have you ever believed or questioned that there was something wrong with you?	
Do you feel like you are missing something or that there is something you don't have and believe that others do?	
Do you feel broken and want to be fixed?	
Do you think you should be able to figure it out?	
Do you think it shouldn't be this hard?	
Do you think others already have it figured out and do it easily?	
Have you been told before that you're not good at something?	
Have you kept yourself from dreaming big because you say, "Why bother?"	
Do you frequently quit on yourself and feel tired of failing?	
Have you ever thought, "If only I could be like (fill in the blank). She's got it all together."?	

Conclusions: There are a lot of chapters that will specifically help you with this obstacle of motherhood. Pay particular attention to the principles shared in Chapter 4 and the entirety of Part 2 where we specifically detail the process of calling on faith, connecting to yourself, and finding confidence in your role as a mom.

The thoughts we have about ourselves, our flaws, our strengths, and our many hats we wear as a mom matter. The core of my process addresses this vital piece of our existence. If you had even one 'Y' (though I know many moms who mark 'Yes' to all of the above), I want you to know that I see you, and I believe in you. You are a great mom. If you have a hard time believing that, stay with me through Chapter 10.

I am overwhelmed with no relief in sight.

A mom's plate is always full and usually cold.

Most of the moms that come to me have incredible demands on their time, like supporting their husband, driving their children to activities, helping with homework, cleaning the house, folding the laundry, cooking meals, doing dishes, changing diapers, and coordinating naptime (for my early year mamas!), and I'm sure I've left off a majority of your to-do list.

We wear so many hats as moms. Sometimes, multiple hats at the same time! How many times have you mediated a sibling tiff in the middle of being your family's chef?

So often, what happens is our overwhelm creeps up on us. We valiantly go from task to task without much room in between to grab a snack, let alone reflect on if there is a better way.

Our time can feel so constricted as moms. You take care of everyone else, and I know that it often feels like you have no time for yourself.

In Chapter 11, I speak specifically about time management for moms.

Self-Assessment	
Instructions: How often do you think these thoughts? Quick take: Give yourself a score for each item between 0-5. 0 = never and 5 = multiple times a day. More in depth: Keep a tally each time you think these types of thoughts to yourself throughout the course of 2-3 days. Use the chart below as examples to inform your self-study.	
There is too much to do.	
I'm spread too thin.	
I'll never take care of it all.	
My to-do list is never ending.	
I need help.	
I'm the one that has to do it all.	
I don't see an end in sight.	
I'm drowning.	

<table>
<tr><td colspan="1">I just want to crawl under the covers and hide all day.</td><td></td></tr>
<tr><td colspan="2">

Initially, I had some nice and tidy score patterns here. 0-14 = you're doing great and managing time and stress. 15-28 = you feel the heaviness of time management while still maintaining your cool and sanity...

But, I realized something.

Just because your score is lower doesn't make it okay to think, "I'll never take care of it all," any amount of times during the week because every thought pattern, positive or negative, greatly impacts the actual outcomes you are producing.

If you feel like you're drowning, whether it's every day or once every few months, I have tools and strategies to help you, starting with Chapter 11.

Being a mom requires an intense amount of management over time, resources, and people. It is possible to feel calm, confident, and in control in regards to your time and your to-do list.

</td></tr>
</table>

"I'll feel better when..."

This phrase is the biggest trap I see when coaching.

We are so overwhelmed with tasks, projects, kids, marriage, and chores... it can be easy - and even seem logical! - to assume that once the outside storm is quiet, we'll feel better.

This is, in fact, not a true statement.

"When [event] is finished, things will be calm again," is the perfect setup for disappointment in your future.

Instead, we can learn how to harness our God-given power to feel better *now*, not after soccer season, not when your mother-in-law finally respects you, and not when your husband finally takes a hint and whisks you away to Hawaii.

You can feel better today before anything else in your life works out.

Self-Assessment	
Instructions: Below are some examples of answers I get from the mamas I coach. Mark an 'X' next to any that resonate with you. I've also left you a few empty spaces if you'd like to fill in any of your own answers.	
"I'll feel better/be happy when..."	
I finally get some sleep.	
I lose some weight.	
I have a lot more money.	
I finish all the things I have to get done today.	
Other people finally change.	
The kids start doing what I ask them to the first time.	
I feel fulfilled in my daily tasks.	
It's the weekend.	

I get a vacation.	
My husband starts paying more attention to me.	
My job recognizes how hard I work and gives me a raise.	
I start praying more.	
The house is all cleaned up.	
My mother-in-law stops saying rude things.	
Conclusion: There are a few elements to finding calm in the present moment, but the beginning of the process is revealed in Chapter 4. For now, I want to impress on you that you have the power within yourself to create the life you want, the life God intends you to live, and you can build it without having to wait for anybody else to show up and make it happen. You've got this, and I've got you.	

I don't control my day. My day controls me.

Not feeling in control ties straight into feeling overwhelmed and overworked but with a slight twist.

This subset of feeling overwhelmed leaves you feeling steamrolled by your to-do list. Feeling powerless is a daily occurrence against the onslaught of requests coming your way.

What's more, if you were given the gift of being still and having some time to refuel yourself and I asked you, "What do you actually want?"...could you answer?

Many of my mamas freeze when asked any variation of this simple question. "I've never thought about that before," or, "I haven't had the time to stop and think about it," is the general reply.

Do you have personal or professional goals that aren't tied to your relationships or your role as a mom?

It can be easy to get wrapped up in your role as mom. Sometimes, we forget that there is a person underneath all of the "mom hats."

Self-Assessment	
Instructions: Ask yourself each question, and indicate a 'Y' for yes or an 'N' for no.	
Do you make a plan but fail to follow through?	
Are you easily distracted?	
Do you have different, pretty planners but give up filling it out after a week?	
Do you say you're going to do the work but when the time comes you make an excuse?	
Do you find all the reasons why now is not the time?	

Do you find it difficult to say 'no' when people ask you to do something you don't really want to do?	
Do you spin on the thought that you don't know where to start?	
Do you feel like you don't have enough time on your hands?	
Do you spend your day on things you *have* to do versus things you *want* to do?	
Do you wish you had more time?	
Are you waiting for the next shoe to drop?	
Before bed, do you think of all the things you didn't get done instead of what you completed throughout your day?	
Would you say you're spending the time on what's important to you?	
Do you make your wants and desires a priority each day?	
Do you feel like you are living in your head instead of living in the moment?	
Do you spend your time wishing things were different?	

Conclusions: If these questions resonate with you, pay particular attention to Chapters 8 and 11 where we clarify your goals and help you set a course that isn't hijacked by the demands on your day.

For now, make sure you give yourself a pat on the back at the end of your day for all you accomplished. It doesn't matter if you only got two things off of your to-do list (or none). You took care of yourself and/or others. You showed up! You lived this day. Give yourself all of the credit and grace. I can't wait to teach you more later in Chapter 8.

I find it difficult to make decisions.

Many moms face the conundrum of feeling stuck because they don't know what the "right" choice is in a given instance.

This aspect is a huge portion of my coaching for some moms, especially because this is a top result I have seen from my own coaching journey.

Needing to know the "right" path is also tied to perfectionism, which we address in Chapter 12.

For now, my basic advice is that every single parent faces uncertainty. The best thing you can do is make your best guess and start going.

If you deem it wrong once you choose, then you learn from it and move on. That's a win! You tried something new and learned that it wasn't for you, ultimately clarifying what *is* for you.

It is my goal to eradicate the phrase "I don't know" from your vocabulary. Confusion keeps you frozen. Get out of feeling stuck by making your best guess and learning from it.

Self-Assessment	
Instructions: Ask yourself each question, and indicate a 'Y' for yes or an 'N' for no.	
Do you feel stuck?	
Are you confused about what to do next?	
Do you spend a lot of time on Google and research the best ways to do things?	
Do you wish you knew how things would turn out beforehand?	
Do you think there's a right or best choice to be made?	
Do you ask everybody else their opinions on things?	
Do you give yourself a lot of time to make the right decisions?	

Do you think that there are big and small decisions and that big decisions need more time?	
Do you keep a lot of things because you might need them later?	
Do you put off deciding things until it's the right time?	
Do you wait to hear what God says before choosing something?	
Conclusion: If indecision is your Achilles' heel, you'll enjoy Chapters 4 and 5 about our thought patterns and the way our brains are designed to work. This knowledge may help you gain greater confidence by understanding how your decision-making process is influenced by the way your brain works. For now, it's helpful to uncover what thought patterns you currently hold. These questions are designed to help you get to know your decision-making tendencies. You have the power to make choices independent of Google's top strategy or your mother-in-law's advice. You are a co-creator with God. Through the strategies I share with you in this book, you can add decision-making to the list of skills that will help you ultimately live a calm, peaceful, and balanced life.	

Chapter 3 Key Takeaways

- The five most common obstacles my moms face are:

    - Feeling like they are broken, ashamed, or that something is wrong with them. If this resonates with you, pay particular attention to Chapters 4 and 10.

    - Feeling overwhelmed and burnt out. If this resonates with you, stay with me through Chapter 11.

    - Constantly thinking, "I'll feel better when…" If this is you, Chapter 4 will be very helpful for you.

    - Feeling like you have no control over your day. If you feel like this with any regularity, Chapters 8 and 11 will be the best help for you.

    - Feeling like you can't make decisions with ease. Chapters 4 and 5 will lay a great foundation for this skill.

CHAPTER 4:

The Key to Feeling Better

Be transformed by the renewal of your mind.
~Romans 12:2

Why do we try new things, set goals, or strive to be better than we were yesterday?

There are a lot of good answers out there... "I want to be proficient in a new skill. I want to lose 15 pounds to fit into my favorite pair of jeans. I want to improve because that is what God has asked."

Like I said, these are good answers, but are not actually the case.

We strive because of the feeling it gives us. When we hit that goal or fit into our old pair of jeans or really feel aligned with God's purpose, we feel good.

We strive and try only to fall down and get back up again because we chase that good feeling.

After learning what I have around the reason why we ever want something in the first place, I feel passionate and motivated to share this with every mom I can. I listen to my friends in their difficult, mom moments, and I know I have the framework, which feels like having the secret sauce, that can help them.

I can't just keep that to myself.

The number one part of this framework is this simple principle: **your thoughts create your feelings,** not the other way around.

The power is within your own brain. Patterns of thought and what you grew up believing to be true for yourself is literally optional. Every thought is an optional thought.

True control lies within you, not whether or not you have enough money in your bank account, what the scale says, or whether your kids are listening to you.

Take this example. How many times have you told yourself you are going to be on your phone less when your kids are around? Your goal is to pay more attention and to be more present with your family. You feel guilty for showing up with a phone in your hand all of the time, and you're determined to change that.

So, you set timers and reminders. You set your phone down. You tell yourself you're not going to feel guilty today, and you probably do a great job with it.

But, it doesn't stick. You have a bad day, and you're on your phone. You turn off an alarm because you're waiting for an important text or phone call. "It's just this one time," you tell yourself. Yet, the phone use creeps back into your after-school routine, and the guilt creeps back into your soul.

Being more present with your kids isn't deciding to put your phone away. If you take action without the right thinking and feeling behind it, your actions will fall short.

I realized this connection and started asking myself why we couldn't just change our lives with action. That's something I've heard throughout my life. It was a difficult concept to let go of.

What finally clicked was learning more about how God created our brains to operate.

Whenever you have a thought, neurons fire in your brain and create neural pathways, like trails through your brain. When you think the same thought again, those same neurons fire and deepen that initial neural pathway. Over time, your brain becomes full of grooves from all of the repeated thoughts in your mind. The more worn the trails, the more that thought has fired in your brain.

These thoughts create such strong neural pathways that they become our belief systems. This system starts when we are young.

If you grew up in a home where your parents didn't have a lot of money and you witnessed coupon cutting and being told there isn't enough money, you have thoughts about money being scarce. As you grow older, those neural pathways deepen. By the time you are an adult, money scarcity is just how the world works. It's now an integral part of your belief system about how the world around you operates.

When a person with this belief system thinks about money being scarce, how do you think they feel?

What I see in my clients is a feeling of there not being enough within the world, their jobs, or within themselves. There's fear in someone with a money scarcity mindset, and there is often shame that they cannot help themselves or their family as they would like to.

Can you see how carrying around these feelings of shame and of there not being enough would shape the actions they take?

If you address the feelings without first addressing the thoughts that first formed that belief, you're not going to change anything long-term.

It all starts with your thoughts.

What can be difficult is gaining awareness of what exactly your thoughts are. Oftentimes, the gap between a thought and the following feeling is so small we don't even notice it. All we know is that we don't feel good.

We remember a time where we felt better, and we start to chase that good feeling. We do our best to follow a pattern of actions to bring that good feeling back.

You might get that good feeling for a moment, but it fades, and you start the cycle over again.

Are you seeing the pattern here?

Thoughts → Feelings → Actions

This is the number one concept I hope you take away from this book.

Your thoughts create your feelings. Your feelings drive your actions.

The biggest thing I help my mamas with in coaching is awareness, and it's something that's almost impossible to do on your own. It's difficult to be aware of what your actual belief system is and what you're thinking to support that belief system, even if that group of beliefs about the world isn't serving you.

Where I stumbled in my journey was the next step, accepting that I was causing my own results of feeling frustrated and overwhelmed. I wasn't owning it because I didn't know that my thoughts created my feelings. Instead, I threw around a lot of blame. Blame for the contractors, blame for my job, blame for the kids when they didn't follow directions, and blame for myself when I didn't workout or when I ate a whole sleeve of cookies.

I refused to own that I was the one choosing this.

Once you're able to accept the reality that you are choosing these feelings, that the way you're looking at your life is optional, then you're able to adjust.

This system of gaining awareness of your own thinking, taking responsibility for being the one who is choosing your thinking, and then being the one to adjust your thinking if you want a different result is the common thread through all of my coaching sessions. It is the secret key that unlocks those feelings you wanted back from Chapter 1.

I empower moms to choose their feelings by helping them gain awareness and acceptance of their thoughts. If you are looking for a neutral, third party who understands you, has real, life-changing tools to share with you, and will support and guide you in this process, please book a time to chat with me here: https://www.daniellethienel.com/my-calendar-page.

I can't promise that it will be an easy process, but I can promise you that you won't be alone on the journey, and this process is what is necessary to take on inside of your mind if you want your life to start changing right now.

Before we move on, I want you to know that not understanding this process until now is not your fault. This is not a process anyone is taught. Like I said before, I felt duped when I first learned this system because no one had ever pointed this out to me before.

I'll explain more about this concept in the next chapter.

If you are feeling ready for help accepting and adjusting your thoughts and your life so you can maximize your motherhood and feel more peace, you can get in touch with me here: https://www.daniellethienel.com/my-calendar-page.

Chapter 4 Key Takeaways
• Your thoughts create your feelings, not the other way around. Challenge: Choose a memory of your life when you felt really happy. Focus your thoughts to take you back to that time. Picture it in your mind and think about all the details. Can you feel the happiness and sadness of that moment right now too? Your thinking is what is making you feel happy right now.
• True control lies within you. Your brain is merely a tool. It is THE tool that God provided to us so we can co-create our lives with Him while here on Earth.

- Repeated thoughts deepen neural pathways that create our belief systems. To reveal what some of your own belief systems are, I recommend doing a thought download. This is where you take out a piece of paper and write down subject headings that you want to explore such as yourself, family, time, home, work, money, etc., and write down all the things about them that you believe are true. This will reveal some of your belief systems around those subjects.

- Thoughts create feelings. Feelings create actions. What do you do when you feel joy? What do you not do when you feel stuck? Can you see the difference in the actions we take when we feel positive things versus negative things?

- Here are the common threads throughout the system I teach: gaining awareness and acceptance of your own thinking patterns, taking responsibility for the thoughts you choose, and learning the skills to adjust your thinking patterns. The process is simple. However, it's not easy to implement ourselves, but with some guidance, you can make it be something that comes more naturally to you.

CHAPTER 5:

Understanding Your Greatest Tool

For God has not given us the spirit of fear; but of power,
and of love, and of a sound mind.
~ 2 Timothy 1:7

The greatest tool for your quest to become a calm, in control, and confident mom is understanding the science behind your brain.

Before we dive in, it must be said that I am not a doctor. This is not high-level neuroscience. This is the explanation that helps me coach you. Stick with me. I'll make this easy to understand, and it's important to know.

Especially for those of you who feel like there is something wrong with you when you can't act the way you want to all of the time. Any mamas who feel like you're broken and need to be fixed...this chapter is going to be especially helpful for you!

For our purposes in this book, we're going to address two main parts of the brain: your higher brain, also referred to as your "boss" brain, and your survival brain, also referred to as your "lizard" brain.

Higher Brain

Your higher brain is in your prefrontal cortex. This is where planning takes place and is the part of your brain that consciously and intentionally makes decisions. We sometimes call this the "boss" brain because anytime you show up and take charge of your life, this is the part of your brain that fires.

This concept of having a higher brain is responsible for the section of my title to step into your "God-given power." This part of your brain is more deliberate.

You can engage this part of your brain with reason and logic. Make a plan. Do a puzzle. Read an article. Solve a problem. Any and all of these activities can help intentionally engage your higher brain.

Survival Brain

Your survival brain is primal, and it's important to understand that the purpose of our survival brain dates back to the beginning of evolution. This part of our brains served us to keep us safe, to survive, and to propel the human race forward. This part of our brains motivates us in three ways: to seek pleasure, avoid pain, and conserve energy.

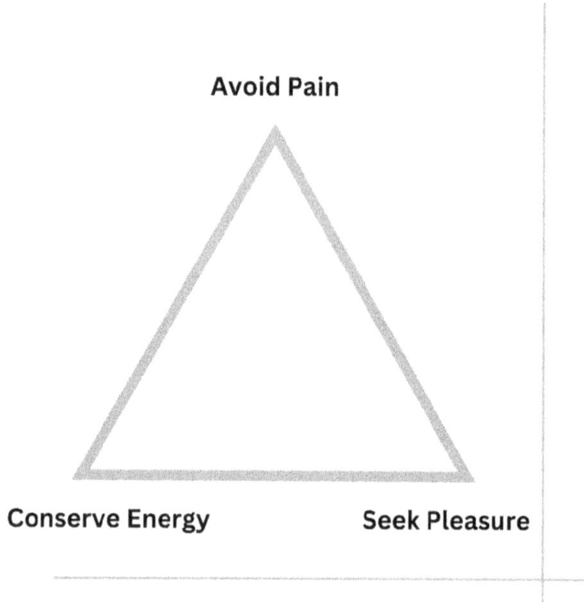

When you think about it, these three things make sense in the context of our survival. We call these three aspects of the survival brain the Motivational Triad because these are the primal motivations we experience as human beings.

The natural reaction is to knock the Motivational Triad as a lesser way of living. Instead, I like to think about it in the context that it was also created by God and is pretty useful in helping humans survive long enough to bring about God's work.

Seeking pleasure equates to procreation. Thanks to this part of the survival brain, we have a human race today.

Avoiding pain is pretty self-explanatory in a survival context. Don't eat those berries. They'll hurt your stomach! Watch out for the sharp-toothed bear. He'll hurt you!

Conserving energy might seem an odd addition when you think about our modern-day lives, but when our ancestors lived in caves, it helped them survive to store a whole bunch of fat on their bodies and not move very much so they could survive the winter.

Bringing the Brain into Modern Day

Understanding that you have separate parts of your brain is vital to your success here.

Now, instead of helping you avoid dangerous situations and hibernating through Winter, your survival brain can kick in and keep you from reaching your goals.

There is a Walgreens on every corner. As soon as you twist your ankle, you can head right on over, slap on some analgesic cream, wrap it in an ACE bandage, and use a crutch to help get out of that pain.

When you get a craving for chocolate because, "Man, do I need some pleasure right now," you can get in the car and, within two minutes, have your chocolate prize.

What about conserving energy? "Well, hello Amazon two-hour delivery. I'm out of groceries." You don't even have to get up off of the couch, and all of a sudden your fridge is full.

These are not bad examples. It can be pretty useful because who doesn't like saving time in making a trip to the store sometimes? But, what happens when we let this part of our brains be in charge of our lives?

Your brain says, "Don't start that business. It's going to be embarrassing, and you're going to have to learn how to deal with technology! You'll be up late and get less sleep. Don't you know it's going to be hard? You'll be criticized and get hate comments. But, you know what? You could be absolutely wrong about everything. Go hang out at the pool. Go enjoy yourself. You don't have to work."

This inner dialogue was exactly what I heard when starting my life coaching business. My survival brain was trying to convince me to avoid pain (you'll be criticized), seek pleasure (oh, just relax. You are always working. Go hang out at the pool), and conserve energy (go find an easier job that doesn't require you to learn a lot of new, hard things).

This knowledge can make all of the difference.

Imagine the difference it would make when you lose it with your kids, instead of self-destructing into the inner "I'm a horrible mom," chant, you could say, "Sorry kids. I listened to my survival brain. Let's try that again."

When you understand this vital difference in your brain anatomy, you can not only start to recognize what part of your brain is holding the reins but consciously tap into your higher brain to step into your power to then go after what you do want to have in your life.

Chapter 5 Key Takeaways

- Your brain is the greatest tool in your toolbox in becoming a Cyclone Mom.

- The two areas of the brain we discussed are the higher brain, or boss brain, and the survival brain, or lizard brain.

- The higher brain utilizes reason and logic. Tapping into this part of the brain is what helps you step into your God-given power. This is where planning takes place. When you are deliberate and intentional with your life, you operate from your higher brain. Take a moment to consciously decide on one thing you will do today. Decide when you will do it. That is tapping into your higher brain.

- The survival brain operates off of the "Motivational Triad." It motivates us to seek pleasure, avoid pain, and conserve energy. The next time you change your mind about doing something you said you wanted to do, can you see that the survival brain came into play, motivating you to not do the hard thing?

- Understanding these functions of the brain make it easier for us to identify which part of our brains is holding the reins and to make conscious choices accordingly.

CHAPTER 6:

We All Need a Coach

I shall ask the Father, and He will give you another advocate to be with you forever.
~John 14:16

Everything begins with a thought. Your internal world determines your external world.

This is true for everyone.

The first person who said, "Huh, is there a better way to provide light than burning candles?" started internally and then pursued the answer externally.

Think about yourself. The wonderful person reading this book. Your brain and heart are inside of your body. Your emotions happen on the inside.

If I just met you on the street, I would have no idea what your life has been like up until now - but you sure do! - because it lives inside of you. You know your history and have years of belief systems built up about all kinds of life subjects. You are also so energetically infused with people who you are with most often in your life.

A metaphor I use to explain this concept, as well as how clearly we see ourselves, goes as follows: it's like you're inside of a jar, and on the outside of the jar are the label, instructions, and directions to follow.

When you're inside of the jar, like you are "inside of your life," you can't read anything that's on the outside.

Could you learn to maneuver and decipher the backwards writing of the label on the outside of the jar and figure it out from the inside of the jar? Yes. It takes a lot of work, but it is possible.

You could also simply hand the jar to someone else who has the skills to read and decipher and ask them what your jar has written on it.

The difference here is the crossroad between doing your own work privately and involving a coach who knows the way and can show you how without you having to figure it all out on your own.

What I'm trying to impart here is that if you want clear results faster, easier, and with less stress and pain than the DIY route, you need to find a life coach. Hiring your own life coach will increase your levels of satisfaction in all of life's different areas. **They also help you unlock the potential your life has that you haven't even come close to tapping into yet.**

Coaching has been vital to the results I have in my own life.

My very first coaching session was 15 years ago. I remember sitting at a table at Whole Foods and being honest with her about how I hated everything that had to do with cooking, shopping, planning, and making meals. This aspect of motherhood was not something that I grew up doing or something my mom helped to welcome me into.

My belief system was, "This is my job. I'm the mom." My husband was working outside of the home. So, it made sense that my job was all the parts of taking care of the home and everything around taking care of the kids, which in my mind, included some of the things that I really didn't like to do.

I felt stuck and felt horrible that I hated it. I should have loved it. This was my job!

My coach listened and prompted lasting change with a simple line of questioning. "Have you ever talked to your husband about it? Can you imagine that this is something you don't have to do? What is the upside to not figuring out an alternative that feels better for you? What if there was another way?"

It broke my brain right open onto the floor of Whole Foods.

I had never even paused to ponder that there were other options out there.

In my conversation with my husband later, he heartily agreed to help with some of the things I hated doing, and he's done them ever since. We're talking about a decade and a half of change from one coaching session. Such a simple insight forever changed the trajectory of what I do on a daily basis.

However, recall back to the beginning of the book. Even though that first session had an incredible impact on my motherhood, I still struggled with blaming others for my happiness. I told myself, "When [this thing happens], I'll feel calm again." I did a little bit of work on my own and got one great result, but still there was so much more, and I still wasn't living my best life.

This is how we work as human beings.

You can't just go to the gym once and have this whole new, beautiful, strong body. You're undoing all of the food, calories, and sugar you've eaten. You don't eat like that for a year and then go to the gym once and call it good.

It's the same process with our brains. Having a coach is going to the mental gym. Your brain is always going, constantly taking in information and forming thoughts.

One coaching session, reading one book, or one day of working on it isn't going to change the way your brain is currently wired.

It takes time to build new muscles and stay focused on what you want to think about yourself, your motherhood, and your goals.

You'll see progress after your first session just like I did, but if that's all you put into your system, it'll wear off. You'll forget, and your years of thinking patterns will take over. Coming to coaching on a regular basis is key to becoming calm, confident, and in control because there is a lot we coaches do to retrain your brain.

There are many options for life coaches that can help you, my friend. Of course, I would love to work with you, but I would rather you work with any coach than none at all.

Ask yourself these questions:

- How fast do you want to get to your goals?

- How do you want to feel along the way?

- Do you want to feel more positive the majority of the time?

- How will you make progress if there's vital knowledge that you're missing? What's the best way to learn that knowledge?

I know how to read the directions on the outside of your jar. I have the training to ask the right questions so I can learn what's going on inside of your jar and reflect back to you what's really going on.

There will always be a cyclone swirling around you. Always. It's never going away. As soon as you feel like you've got it all figured out, something else comes into your life and knocks you down if you're not practiced.

This is why I still choose to involve a coach in my life. I love having an expert in my corner on my side, helping me remove the obstacles I can't see myself and providing strategies that carry me to the finish line of my life goals. I will always want to have my own life coach too because, when I do, life becomes smoother to navigate and exponentially more satisfying.

That was the whole thing for me. I always told myself, "I'm smart. I went to college. I've accomplished a lot in my life, and I should be able to figure this out on my own. Why can't I figure out how to have some chill time for myself or not to get so angry with my kids all of the time?"

I was missing these key pieces of vital information. I was missing a coach with life-changing tools and concepts. I needed someone who was trained to hold a non-judgemental and loving space for me to get out all my struggles and challenges so I could receive guidance on what I couldn't change myself.

I was missing someone who could challenge my thoughts and belief systems. No matter what I had tried to do differently in my life, it was like I was trying to do the same things over and over again, expecting new results each time.

I think you might be missing this, too. A coach who can look at your internal world and concentrate on your brain. A coach who has a blinged out tool-box from which to draw just the right resources to help you change your mindset so you can get different results.

If you would like to explore coaching with me to speed up your results and experience less stress along the way in your busy mom life, click this link and follow the instructions to set up a time for us to chat: https://www.daniellethienel.com/my-calendar-page.

I know this can feel like a lot. I imagine you listening to this as you drive around or reading this in your closet while you sneak a few moments to yourself. It can feel overwhelming when you look at all of the areas in your life you want to see the results of peace and balance.

I want to tell you one thing: don't worry. You don't have to change all of the areas of your life. If you can focus on your mind and what's happening in there, then everything overflows over into your life.

You don't have to run a marathon in order to be fit. You don't have to calm the storm that's raging around you right now. You simply have to go within your mind and heart to find the power you need in order to feel how you want to feel and be who you want to be. Here is where you will have the control to create any experience you want no matter what is swirling around you or coming at you in your life.

In the next section, I'll walk you through my process step-by-step. This isn't meant to replace coaching but to better equip you with the knowledge that will make coaching far more effective to achieve the deep results you want in your life.

Up next is The Cyclone Mom Method.

Chapter 6 Key Takeaways

- Having a coach can get you results faster, easier, and with less stress and pain than the DIY route. What have you already been trying on your own to make the changes you want to see in your life? Is it working for you?

- Coaching has been vital to the results I've gotten in my own life.

- It takes time to build new muscles and stay focused on what you want to think about yourself, your motherhood, and your goals. Coaching is the way to build these new muscles.

- When considering a coach, ask yourself these questions:

    - How fast do you want to get to your goals?

    - How do you want to feel along the way?

    - Do you want to feel more positive the majority of the time?

    - How will you make progress if there's vital knowledge that you're missing?

    - What's the best way to learn that knowledge?

PART 2:

THE CYCLONE MOM METHOD

There are five pillars that we want to concentrate on that will help you achieve the balance and peace that you want in this life of yours right now, whatever stage of motherhood you find yourself in.

CHAPTER 7:

Calling on Your Faith

I can do all things through Christ who strengthens me.
~Philippians 4:13

This is the most vital piece of my framework, which is why it is first.

Whatever your faith is, you can adapt this to work for you. I am a member of the Catholic Church, and I draw on prayer, the sacraments, and what my faith teaches to give me a foundation in my life. This is where I draw my core values from. I ask Christ every day to use me as a channel of His peace and use the gifts He has bestowed on me to connect to other moms out there who are suffering or are just not living the life they want to, and I believe that is why you're here today.

Are you connecting all of the parts of your daily life to your faith? Are you finding the time in your busy schedule to include your faith in your day? Are you calling on your faith so you can improve those areas?

If you are already, great. I want to help you enhance that.

If you find yourself answering with an, "I'm not really being as mindful to bring in my faith to everything as much as I want to," or, "I am not making the time I want to for prayer or deepening my relationship with Christ," then these tips I am going to offer you will help you start connecting more with your faith.

This step of increasing your connection with your faith to your daily life and making the time to prioritize it will undoubtedly lead to a more peaceful and balanced life.

Mindfulness in Faith

In order to enhance your daily life and connect more faith with everything that's going on in your life, you must remember that your thoughts are where your feelings begin. What you cultivate in your mind is important.

Can you bring your thoughts towards Christ today? It takes practice because our minds naturally focus on the task at hand, but you can learn how to be present in a faithful way while simultaneously functioning in your daily life.

It's like there's more than one track running at a time. You'll be able to remain mindful of what you're doing, but you can also dedicate one of those tracks to heaven.

I admit that staying conscious of Him, of Jesus, when I'm busy can be very challenging for me. I'm thankful that he created our minds to function in a way where we can bounce back and forth in the midst of something that is troubling for us.

I want you to give this a try. Say out loud, "Today, as much as I can, I'm going to go about my daily life as I want to."

Then, challenge yourself by saying, "How much can I bring my thoughts to my faith?" All it takes is reading a few lines of scripture, pausing to recite a short prayer, or even a simple act of reaching out such as,"Help me, Jesus," "I trust in you, Jesus," or, "I love you, Jesus" to be mindful.

I have a picture in my office that says, "Holy Spirit, you are welcome here." I love that reminder every time I see it. I wear a Miraculous Medal, and I consciously touch it throughout the day. I can pause in the middle of the hustle and bustle of life and just direct my mind to my faith.

What's the Rush?

I want to question the notion that we need to hurry in order to rush. I find that when many of my clients first come to me, they believe that always being in a hurry is part of life, that that is how it'll always be, or that rushing is what's necessary to get it all done. I want to question this, especially for the mom who feels the little panic and frustration of not having everything done because God is never in a hurry.

When I'm dealing with these feelings of rushing, I ask myself, "What is God's rhythm?"

Think about it. Think about what we know about Christ and His time here on Earth. Does it come to mind that He was ever rushing around or that He had to hurry to get somewhere? No.

How many times did He always put His time to walk off and go by Himself in prayer first? When you think about Him and you think about His nature, He is calm, present, and unhurried. He is slow, thoughtful, and soaks things in.

This is one way I connect my daily life to my faith. When I find myself feeling hurried, in a rush, just a little behind, or wanting to turn up the speed and just get something over with, I call on my faith in this way.

I say to myself, "Okay. I want to be in God's rhythm. What do I need to do? What would that look like for me in this moment if I was moving about as Christ would be?"

It immediately calms me down and removes the self-imposed pressure to say that there is no rush because I am reminded His rhythm is the best rhythm to imitate.

That is something I want to offer you and invite you to try today. If you are able to slow yourself down, then you will enhance your life greatly by calling on this aspect of faith.

Call on Courage

The life of a mom is hard. We face many challenges and, to move through them, will require being brave and having courage. This is the feeling that I've come to know is imperative for us to reach the goals we have for living our best life and the feeling it takes to overcome our biggest obstacles.

How many times has the Lord told us not to be afraid? I believe this is one of the most repeated phrases in the Bible. "Do not be afraid."

I picture those words coming from Christ directly to me into my heart, and it automatically gives me courage.

When you find yourself feeling afraid and fearful, like worrying about your children or feeling anxiety about money, relationships, and whether or not you're doing a good enough job, is the perfect time to call on your faith.

Remind yourself that He tells us, "Do not be afraid," and call upon courage in your life.

You Are Never Alone

In order to get the peace and balance you want, I cannot stress enough that I want you to incorporate this on a daily basis. If you are struggling with loneliness, there are three ways I want to illustrate that you are never alone.

First, our faith in Christ tells us He is present with us at all times. He's right there with you now! I know this because it is said that wherever two or more have gathered, He is there, even in this exchange between you, the reader, and me, the author… He is present.

You can always call upon Him, even when you're feeling lonely. That loneliness comes from not having the focus of where you want to go. From now on, tell yourself, "He is here with me, so I am never alone."

Second, notice how we are born. We are born into a family (even if circumstances are less than ideal) and our families gather in communities. Sprawling communities give way to nations that make up our planet. We were never meant to go it alone!

In fact, modern science backs up this phenomenon with what they call "tribe mentality." The straight definition is "the human tendency to seek out and connect with like-minded people who share common interests, beliefs, or habits."

When you hear another person's story, it allows you to connect with them. Even if only a small principle of their story resonates with you, you feel less lonely. The problems you are dealing with aren't only happening to you. Isolation and shame breed best in the dark. Shine a light by connecting with others in your family and community.

I personally love the team atmosphere. As a professional ballet dancer (which was my first career many years ago now), my favorite performances were ensemble shows. We all had separate parts which had its fun too, but for me, there was nothing quite like the feeling of accomplishment in performing altogether.

Lastly, I know there are times when it's difficult to connect to your family and friends or when a stranger's stories feel a million miles off from what you've experienced.

While you can always know that Christ is there, I know there are times when you can't grasp his presence or feel like he is physically there.

This is when having a coach is vital. You don't have to take on a new, big, scary goal all by yourself! You can have a partner. A guide. This is the exact reason I hired my own life coach to help me. It would take me so much longer, be so much harder, and be way less fun if I were to do this all by myself. I echo my words from Chapter 6: hire a coach.

Our Ultimate Goal

Even though our brains will fight it, we don't know when we are going to die and move on from this world.

It is unknown to us, but we are all going to meet that day at some point.

Going through your life knowing that your ultimate goal is to spend eternity in heaven can bring daily peace.

When you have a circumstance that you're having trouble meeting, a problem you're trying to solve, or a challenge you're having to endure, it's all okay. This is the experience we have on Earth. Ultimately, if I know that I'm on track to go to heaven, that knowledge brings an instant injection of peace and calm into my life. Keeping the destination of eternity as what truly matters releases any heaviness if and when I get caught up in the meaningless intricacies of daily work and life.

When you connect your faith to your daily life, you will have a more peaceful, balanced, and joyful life. You will be mindful of your faith, following a rhythm Christ used in his own life, drawing on courage, remembering you are not alone, and guiding each day with your ultimate goal of eternity.

When you focus on making the necessary shifts in your **internal life**, physical results will then tangibly begin to reflect in your **external life,** allowing you to move more peacefully and joyfully along the journey to **eternal life.**

It is my hope that you can act on these principles starting today and build upon this practice continually. If you want to automatically become the person whose mind is wired to do this regularly, this is the work I help moms do inside my coaching program. I invite you to explore what may be an amazing option for you in your life right now: https://www.daniellethienel.com/my-calendar-page.

Chapter 7 Key Takeaways

- Calling on your faith is the most vital part of my framework.

- Increasing the connection to your faith will lead to more peace and balance.

- Incorporate mindfulness by asking how you can bring your thoughts towards Christ today. Can you think of 3 ways that you can build in more mindfulness towards Christ by the time you go to bed tonight?

- Adopt God's rhythm. Ask yourself, "What would that look like for me in this moment if I was moving about as Christ would be?"

- The Lord has advised us to not be afraid. Take courage in your role as a mom. Do 1 thing today outside of your comfort zone that requires you to be brave. What is the result when you hand over your fear to God to take care of it?

- Remember, you are never alone. He has promised us to be near us always. Also, make a list of 3 people, perhaps including another faith-filled mom, that you could call on when you feel alone.

- Keep in mind your ultimate goal: eternity.

CHAPTER 8:

Clarifying Your Goals

Open your works to the Lord, and your intentions will be set in order. ~Proverbs 16:3

The next part of my framework to help you be a calm, in control, and confident Cyclone Mom is to design your future.

It's time to look ahead and become the designer and creator of what you actually want.

Set your brain to the future. In order to create a roadmap, we need to have a deeper understanding and clarity as to where we are going. We'll also need to get specific and understand the driving force behind our choices.

Sometimes we get swept along in the flow of life. We wait and see where things end up, and that is an option of how you could live your life. There are some things we can choose to be relaxed about.

If you find you fall into this laid-back category, my invitation to you is simply to get curious. Activate curiosity mode in your brain and flow in a direction of getting a little bit clearer about some goals you actually want to set.

Part of stepping into your God-given power and finding more balance and joy is becoming more deliberate about how you're living your life.

This concept of deliberation has woven its way through multiple chapters in this book. It's a powerful notion that carries us to where we want to go.

I want you to think about a GPS system. There are two elements you need in order to properly use a GPS for its intended purpose. You need a current location and a specific address of where you would like to go.

I want you to see that it is necessary for you to decide and get specific about where you want to go in life. Planning ahead of time puts you into gear, utilizing your higher brain, the prefrontal cortex, as we learned back in Chapter 5.

Your Personal Mission

Your first step is one of my favorite exercises. I call this your personal mission statement.

Organizations around the world craft a mission statement to help them remember what is most important in their actions. It's short enough to memorize. It's easy to keep in front of you.

This mission statement is crucial to clarifying your goals. It informs your path forward.

For example, let's say I have a goal of traveling across Europe. I want to see the world, but my personal mission right now is to be present as a mom and attend as many of my children's activities as possible. Can you see how the goal doesn't quite serve my current mission?

Mission statements will shift with each stage of motherhood. Having a personal mission statement crafted will help you get more specific about what goals support the way you want to show up in your life.

Crafting a mission statement helps you to feel less like you're throwing goals on a page willy-nilly and more like each goal you pursue truly aligns with what you want out of this stage of life.

Here is an example:

"It is my personal mission in life to follow God's plan for me as well as love and lift those I interact with. I seek to deepen my marriage through communication and quality time, to take care of my two children with love and quiet answers, and to bring excellence into each project I take on at work. Everything I do points to a life centered around the qualities of Jesus Christ: love, courage, and meekness to name a few. It is my mission that I can live as God would have me live to share His spirit, love, and grace wherever I go."

- Kim, 31-year-old mother

Can you see how Kim's statement would make it easy to discern between two competing choices?

Let's say Kim is offered an incredible opportunity to travel across Europe for a year, but she would have to go alone due to her family's circumstances. Given her mission statement, saying "yes" to this opportunity would make it difficult to deepen her marriage or take care of her two children in the ways she wants to and would be in conflict with the mission statement she wrote for herself. Having a mission statement makes it easier for Kim to decline the invitation and live with purpose.

To write your own personal mission statement, I suggest following three simple guidelines:

1) What responsibilities do you have at this stage in your life? Don't be shy about including all of the hats you are currently wearing. How would you like to show up to these roles?

2) At its core, where is all of this leading you? Is there a common thread or theme you feel represents the life you want to live?

3) Relate your answers to the teachings of Christ and God's plan for your life. How does He tie into your personal mission during this stage?

Goal Setting

Oftentimes, I coach my clients to put pen to paper and write down what your ideal future looks like. Where do you live? How many kids do you have? What kind of school do they go to? How much do you weigh? How do you dress? What vacations are you going on? How much money do you have? What car do you drive? Where do you work?

What I find most often for clients I coach is they can pick out maybe 5-10 things. That is a great start!

Keep asking your brain what else it wants. What else sounds fun? If you had a magic wand, what would you wish for? Have fun with it.

Then, move on to prioritizing what goals you want to go after first. Picking five is good, but three is even better. As we'll discuss in Chapter 11, you can build momentum by choosing a smaller portion of your list to tackle first.

Once you have your 3-5 goals you want to pursue first, your next step is to overcome the obstacles inherent in the journey. You need some strategies in place to help you get to where you want to go.

For example, let's say you choose to focus on a trip to Europe. Maybe your brain is telling you that you don't know if you can get time off of work or perhaps your passport isn't up to date. You can strategize by taking steps to get actual answers about taking time off of work or what the process and timeline are for getting an updated passport.

Take the guesswork out of any obstacle that comes up. This allows you to commit to taking action and actually see progress toward your goals. In the midst of the journey, you see yourself make achievements. You're creating results, which creates a feeling of empowerment, which feeds into achieving more goals.

Like other areas of becoming a Cyclone Mom, this begets a positive cycle of growth and momentum.

Even when you haven't reached the ultimate goal yet but can recognize some progress, I want you to know that you can celebrate the small wins along the way.

This exercise of getting clear on your goals, taking action, and celebrating along the way will help you design and achieve the future that you want.

Have peace of mind that you're on your way. Like you do with your time, evaluate along the way. Make adjustments and celebrate the failures that help you learn just as much as you celebrate your successes.

If you want some help getting clear on where you are now, where you're headed, or help building consciousness over your life to face those obstacles head-on, I can offer you strategies and one-on-one help to celebrate and create together until you've reached your dream future.

This is what I do professionally on a daily basis with other mamas just like you. Mamas who are trying to balance their relationships, their motherhood, and their time. Mamas who feel like that eventual trip to Europe, farmhouse, or peaceful mother-in-law relationship is out of reach.

Whatever your goals are, having an organized home, a regular self-care routine, or starting a side business while you focus on raising your children are not out of your reach. They are ripe for the taking! If you'd like help along your way, please reach out using this link: https://www.daniellethienel.com/my-calendar-page.

Together, we can get started designing the life you've always dreamed of.

Chapter 8 Key Takeaways

- Become a designer and creator of the life you want by clarifying your goals. Make a list of 25 (yes 25!) things you want to experience, feel, do, or achieve. From the list, go through and choose your top 5. Put those 5 in order of what matters most to focus on. Do one thing today toward making progress with your #1 goal.

- Part of stepping into your God-given power and finding more balance and joy is becoming more deliberate about how you're living your life. Take 5 minutes and visualize your life working exactly as you want it to. What are all the specific details of that vision?

- Crafting a mission statement is crucial to clarifying your goals and informs your path forward. Put pen to paper and write down a few notes about your core values and some priorities for the current stage of motherhood you are in. Include 3-5 goals that support your personal mission statement.

- Even when you haven't reached your ultimate goal, celebrate the small victories along the way. How can you begin to enjoy the journey however near or far you are to your goal?

CHAPTER 9:

Connecting with Yourself

The Kingdom of God is within you. ~Luke 17:21

This part of my framework elevates the relationship you have with yourself.

First, we want to discover what current beliefs you have about yourself. This is essential before we do anything else. Many of us keep going on with life, birthdays pass and years go by, and we don't stop to reevaluate and ask ourselves, "What do I currently believe about myself?"

And, the important part, "Do I want to keep it, or am I ready to let go of it?"

There is so much that you can find out about yourself. Parts that you love and parts that you believe in.

This work could be the best thing you can do for yourself.

Of course, there can always be room for improvement if you want to focus on it, but I want to focus on your inner voice, which is your thoughts.

What does that voice sound like? Is it criticizing? Is it compassionate? Are you judgemental of yourself or full of self-love?

My guess is you're likely somewhere between those extremes. Are you naturally someone who believes that you're confident and capable? Do you believe you can achieve your dreams, or are you doubtful about your ability?

In my coaching program, we take this a little bit deeper. We examine the biggest fears you have about yourself. We get clear on how you handle both positive and negative life events and what feelings play into your perception of yourself.

An important aspect of doing this for yourself is to take a look at your *values*. Are you using your values as a guide when you talk to yourself? Do your self-beliefs and your values line up with each other?

Especially in moms of faith, I can't stress how often a mom can be compassionate to everyone around her and so distressing in the way she talks to herself. Does the way you speak to yourself align with something you would tell your best friend? If not, then stop saying it to yourself. I urge you to take on the internal speech that would align with something Christ would say to you if you two were sitting down and having a conversation. This notion of speaking to yourself with either love or condemnation is important to catch and to understand.

When you have a relationship with someone else, it takes place in the mind, including what you think about them and what you feel about them. It's the same principle with your own self. **Your relationship with yourself is literally just the thoughts you think about yourself.**

Spend some time in awareness of what that inner voice sounds like. Then, I invite you to consider what is keeping you stuck.

Perfectionism

The first thing that keeps a lot of us stuck when trying to improve our relationship with ourselves is perfectionism. I personally had to redefine this for myself because I had this thought and belief that striving for perfection was a good thing. It helped me to achieve a lot, but in retrospect, what I learned through my own coaching is that perfectionism was holding me back - big time!

I'll write more in depth about this later, but I often talk about aiming for B minus. This concept changed my whole motherhood. Instead of going for a gold star and getting on myself if I didn't show up perfectly, I allowed myself to simply show up and do good enough.

When we are full of the fear of failure, we don't try. We don't go after everything we want and can achieve.

The thought pattern to look for here sounds something like, "I can't do it. I don't know how. I've never done anything like this before. It's not good enough. I might embarrass myself."

Whatever the pattern that is keeping you stuck, we want to identify it so we can get out of our own way because what you really want is progress and results. When we are stuck in perfectionism, we don't make progress or complete things because striving for perfection keeps us exactly in that state of striving so we never arrive at the finish line.

We can adjust from a fear of failure to understanding that we win when we set out for something, whether we get it or we learn from it. Failure helps us learn.

Holding on to the Past

Another aspect of our inner voice that can keep us stuck is struggling with our past, wishing it was different than it was.

In this moment, where all of your power lies, we refer back to what has been and what we've done up until now. We look for what we're capable of today by going back and thinking about our past.

Whatever took place in our past doesn't have any bearing on our future. Only our thoughts about the past that we choose to think about today affect our future. We want to let go of the things in our past that don't help us move forward. We do this by rewriting the story - our collections of thoughts and beliefs - in our minds about what took place.

I use a specific exercise with my clients who struggle with their past. This exercise shifts the narrative and has them become the hero of their past experiences. You get to tell your story any way you want to, and I will always urge you to pick something on purpose that will be life-serving to you.

Refusing to relinquish your past is like carrying this extra, big rock around in your purse. In order to elevate your relationship with yourself, you need to let the rock go. You've got to take it out of your purse and throw it off to the side. You'll feel lighter, be kinder to yourself, and greatly enhance the outcome of your future.

Not Living Your Own Truth

There are two different ways you can block your relationship with yourself in this category.

First, is people pleasing. When we participate in people-pleasing behaviors, we are really lying to ourselves and to the other person we're committing to.

When we say, "Yes! I'll do [thing]," even when we don't really want to, we are not living in our own truth.

We have this idea that if we say no to them, they'll think poorly of us and that you somehow don't qualify to be a good or generous person.

People pleasing doesn't benefit anyone.

The second way we can block our relationship with ourselves by not living our own truth is to live based on what other people think. This usually goes hand-in-hand with people pleasing.

I help clients with this particular problem over and over again. If this is a struggle for you, I urge you to go down the path of elevating this part of your life. It will change everything.

We do not have any control over and cannot change what goes on inside of other people's heads. No matter what we do or say, even if we believe we're doing the right thing, there's no controlling the reaction inside of someone else.

Instead of making choices based on other people's thoughts, I help my mamas come back and live an authentic life where what matters most is what you think about your own self.

To start, stop using the word "should." I call this "should-ing." There's not much benefit from the thoughts that spring from "should." Starting with "should" automatically creates a heaviness and pressure that will always stop you from being the best version of yourself.

A Lack of Boundaries

Many times, when a client first comes to me, they'll say something like, "I just need to make better boundaries." They believe that these boundaries need to be set for their children, inlaws, or boss to follow.

I see this and ask, "Are you establishing boundaries that work for you?"

There's a slight miss here for many of my clients. Whenever you make a boundary, it is about you. For example, what you will and won't allow or what you will and won't do if a request you've made isn't followed.

When helping clients with time management, it is essential to set and uphold boundaries in order to prioritize schedules and complete work tasks, chores, and daily to-do's. The focus, however, is on you and your follow-through that really has you taking control of your time. More on this later in Chapter 11. Becoming a better setter and follower of our own boundaries can really elevate your relationship with yourself.

As you take a look at your current beliefs and thoughts about yourself, keep an eye out for perfectionism, holding on to the past, not living your own truth, and lacking proper boundaries. These are important topics that create a pathway for you to move from feeling overwhelmed and busy to living your greatest potential.

<table><tr><td>

Chapter 9 Key Takeaways

- An important aspect of becoming a Cyclone Mom is addressing the relationship you have with yourself.

- Take a look at your values. Are you using your values as a guide when you talk to yourself? Do your self-beliefs and your values line up with each other?

- Your relationship with yourself is literally just the thoughts you think about yourself.

- There are four areas that can hold you back from having a healthy relationship with yourself:

  - **Perfectionism.** We can adjust from fear of failure to understanding that we win when we set out for something, whether we get it or we learn from it. What are you currently trying to do perfectly?

  - **Holding on to the past.** You get to tell your story any way you want to, and I will always urge you to pick something on purpose that will be life-serving to you. Rewrite the story of the past where you are the HERO of the story. How is it different from what you tell yourself now? Do you see how this new way of telling the story of your past will serve your life going forward?

  - **Not living your own truth.** Instead of making choices based on other people's thoughts, I help my mamas come back and live authentic lives where what matters most is what they think about themselves.

</td></tr></table>

- **A lack of boundaries.** Whenever you make a boundary, it is about you. For example, what you will and won't allow. Pick one area of your life where you want to have more boundaries. What would it solve for you if you were to follow through on your boundary?

CHAPTER 10:

Confidently Be Mom

I have told you this so you may have peace in me. In the world you will have trouble, but take courage, I have conquered the world. ~John 16:33

This part of the Cyclone Mom Method centers around understanding your role of mother.

First, I'd like to point out something seemingly obvious. You are a mother, but it's also separate from you as the person you are.

Being a mom is your function, position, responsibility, and vocation. It's not all wrapped into one when it comes to who you are. The "mom" part is only part of your capacity.

The goal within this step of my framework is to maximize your role as a mom. I want you to show up ten times more effectively than you currently are if you want to.

I want you to notice that I mention the importance of elevating your relationship with yourself (Chapter 8) before we talk about motherhood. Elevating your own inner relationship makes this part easier because being a mom is only one part of who you are, and when you exquisitely take care of and connect with yourself first, you will automatically enhance how you show up as a mom.

You Are a Good Mom

At this point, I invite you to own your infinite worthiness.

There's all of this talk about "good mom" and "bad mom," and that just doesn't need to exist. You're here, reading a book about trying to become a calm, in control, and confident mom through your own God-given power.

You exist. You were breathed into life from God. By this divine law of existence, you are 100% worthy. That's a fact, and so is the truth that you can't get any more worthy than you already are because you are infinitely worthy.

You also are a good mom. There isn't an upside to believing anything but this. Don't allow yourself to question it anymore. It's a choice, and when you choose to focus on faults, mistakes, and not seeing your humanness, you fall prey to a false belief that you aren't good.

The other option is to take on a lighter attitude that will serve your motherhood a thousandfold. Two of my personal favorite thoughts or phrases that help me and my clients ground ourselves in truth and not question our "good enoughness" are:

1) "There I go being human again."

2) "I am both amazing and a mess."

This reminds me that I am divinely made yet am having a human experience. I invite you to adopt these mom mindset conditioners as often as necessary too.

Imagine what would change if you didn't question whether or not you were worthy of the title of "good mom." It's just a constant truth.

Accepting this fact is the first step to maximizing your role as a mom.

Prioritize Self-Care

Self-care matters. It matters so much, and I want to, right off the bat, dispute the idea that self-care is selfish.

By definition, a selfish act puts others in harm's way. You taking great care of yourself is anything but harmful. In fact, it benefits everyone you encounter.

So, if you are doing something that is good for you, that you want to be doing, and that makes you feel good and your brain thinks, "This is selfish," then check in with yourself. "Am I putting somebody in harm's way because of this?"

That is a simple way to either quiet your brain or take action in alignment with who you want to be.

Most likely, it's not selfish. At least not from all of the examples I have in the moms I coach.

Taking care of yourself is going to fill yourself up and give yourself the energy to show up as the mom you want to be! That love you show yourself overflows and becomes more love that you are able to give to your family and those around you.

This principle of self-care also ties into your worth. Everything is based on this: you are worthy. You are a good mom. Good moms take care of themselves. When good moms prioritize their own care, they are better able to take care of those around them.

It's a beautiful cycle of love. Since we already know that you are infinitely worthy, you are worthy of participating in the self-care cycle.

When we prioritize self-care, we also build our self-confidence. It helps us feel better. When you feel better, you do better. Self-care will help you maximize your role as a mom, because you then take the actions necessary to carry out being the mom you dream of being.

There is another version of you. One where your mental and emotional health is soaring. One where your physical and spiritual well-being is filled to the brim. It all starts with believing that filling your cup, prioritizing self-care, and putting yourself on the to-do list while making it mandatory to check off is actually the roadmap to all you dreamed of when you became a mom.

Expand Your Emotional Wellness

Living through a global pandemic in your lifetime highlights the importance of physical wellbeing. We focus on washing our hands, getting enough rest, and eating nutritious foods that make our bodies strong.

In my program, we focus on emotional health. From Chapter 4, you know what feelings are, where they come from, and how they're created.

I'll go more in depth on this principle later, but I coach on a principle that is called the 50/50. The punchline of this tool is that negative feelings are okay and to be expected. Negative emotions are also a sign that your life is on track. Again, I go more into depth on the 50/50 later. We don't have to avoid, react to, or resist negative emotions. We have to learn how to process them (which we discuss more in Chapter 9).

If that sounds foreign to you, I promise it isn't as hard or difficult to learn as it sounds. The key to emotional health is learning how to allow negative feelings and how to process them. Expanding your emotional wellness will help you maximize your role as a mother because you won't be as caught up in battling your emotions. You'll know what to do with them.

What I'm offering you here is the pathway to more peace, balance, and joy in your mom life. When you feel guilty, worried, or overwhelmed, how differently would your day play out if you possessed the skill to accept and process that emotion? If you learned how to be gentle with yourself, wouldn't that change how you show up as a mom?

A lot of moms come to me with their top feelings on a daily basis being some combination of overwhelm, anxiety, stress, defeat, and tiredness. What would change when these feelings weren't in the top three but instead the bottom ten of what you felt on a daily basis? This is the change that is available to you and what I help my clients with daily.

Become clear on where you are buffering in your life.

By this, I mean gain awareness on when you are avoiding feeling uncomfortable feelings by getting a quick dopamine hit. You could be avoiding feelings with food, sugar, alcohol, or drinking – anything you use to escape from the feelings of stress and overwhelm.

We want to pay particular attention to this behavior because it accomplishes the opposite of what we want it to. We don't show up at maximum capacity when we avoid our emotions. For example, when we shove our emotions "under the rug" or when we resist our emotions as if we're trying hard to "hold a beach ball underwater." The ball eventually bursts up out of the water and it makes an even bigger splash than if we let the ball just rise gently to rest on the surface.

Buffering is something I address often in my coaching. Seeing that it is possible to stop, process, and participate in our favorite experiences because we want to, not because we don't know how to handle our negative emotions, is key to going after our dreams.

Be Deliberate About Enjoying Motherhood

Whatever stage you're going through, there are things you can find joy in.

I know it can sound so difficult, especially when you have a new baby and you're up all night, or you're navigating a disability with a child, or you're having a difficult time with your teenager, or you have children growing up and moving out.

That's the stage I'm in now. My twin daughters are in college, and my son has his driver's license now. I've learned that I don't have to stop maximizing my role as their mom, even when they aren't physically under my roof or have more independence. I am, now and forever, their mother, and there are things I can find joy in during this stage of my motherhood.

Yes, there are particular circumstances in this stage of motherhood that are very challenging.

Yes, your day-to-day can be hard. What I want you to lean on is that there are also some very special and wonderful things about the particular stage of motherhood you are in right now, and your brain is just not focused on these positives enough.

Before you know it, your kids will grow, and different circumstances and challenges will arise, so don't leave one stage and enter another before you've soaked every ounce of goodness out of your current stage. Right now, I don't have a little, soft cheek to cuddle up in my lap and press into my own face, but I do have time to just pick up and go somewhere with ease. Don't miss what's great about the present because your joy and your power is only found in the here and now.

Don't delay. Enjoy the journey. Find what is great about now because it will pass.

This ability to be deliberate about what you are enjoying is a gamechanger. It strengthens your mindset and will help you maximize your role as a mom.

Chapter 10 Key Takeaways

- Maximizing your role as a mother is the next step in becoming a Cyclone Mom.

- You are a good mom. Own your infinite worth.

- Prioritizing self-care is not selfish. It is essential. Make a list of 15 self-care activities, both big and small, so you will always be able to remind yourself what to do to take extreme care of yourself.

- Expand your emotional wellness. You don't have to avoid, react, or resist negative emotions. In Chapter 13, you'll learn the process of what you can do instead.

- Be deliberate about enjoying motherhood. Don't delay. Enjoy the journey. Find what is great about now because it will pass. Name 5 wonderful things about the stage of motherhood you are in right now and especially look for things that won't be a part of a future stage.

CHAPTER 11:

Control of Your Time

*For everything there is a season, and a time
for every purpose under heaven.*
~Ecclesiastes 3:1

The next step of the framework I use to help my clients become Cyclone Moms is moving toward balance, supported by the thought that you have enough time.

In order to instill that belief, I want to show you how you can create more time in your life.

The paradox of time is that you have plenty of time, but you also have a finite amount of time.

If you look at time and money, those are both circumstances. If you run out of money, you can use your brain to go about getting more of it.

But, if you have an hourglass set for your life, you're born with a full bulb of sand, and you will die when the sand runs out. You can't send sand back up through the hourglass. That's not how time works.

So, how can we adopt an abundant mindset about time if we can't approach it the same way we do with our other resources like money?

The Mental Construct of Time

The answer lies in the phenomenon I'm sure you've experienced. You go from day to day and look up to realize a week or month has passed and think to yourself, "Whoa! It's over already? Where did that week go?!"

You weren't conscious about your time. It passed without your awareness.

That is the first step to "create" more time in your life. Become more conscious about what time really is.

We can go through and google the history of time - which is admittedly fascinating - and feel grateful for the organization of hours into days, days into weeks, weeks into months, and so on.

But, this mental construct is often exactly what we allow to get in our way and dictate whether or not we feel like we have plenty of time or none at all.

The first step is to evaluate. Take this past week, or even an upcoming week, and ask yourself what you're spending your time on. This could look like making a list.

Notice what you're doing. Are there things where you think "I have to do this," versus "I get to do this?" Do you choose tasks on purpose? Is there an order of importance to the list in front of you?

I want you to notice if you see something on your list that makes you feel heavy or pressured. Perhaps it's something like grocery shopping. As you dig deeper, you may realize this is something you do want because you like to have food prepared and ready.

In order to expand our time, we need to be reevaluating on a recurring basis if we're aligned with how we're spending our time. Even if there are things on your list like the grocery shopping example, take note of anything that you realize you thought was a drag on your time but you now see as, "I actually do want to figure out how to do this."

Be Deliberate About Your Time

Now, notice the things on your list that you don't want to do or aren't serving a purpose that aligns with you. You have to make a decision to let them go or determine to figure out another way of getting them done. Maybe, they served you in the past. Maybe, they were things you used to want and just became automatic, things your mind accepted as something you just have to do.

These things are from a past version of yourself. If a task doesn't fit your current iteration and who you want to become, give yourself permission to let it go. You get to decide what is best in regards to how you spend your time. Perhaps, you want to keep it as well, like cleaning your house, but instead, you are willing to swap your time for money and hire someone else to do it. Now, you will have created more time for yourself.

The point here is that the choice is yours. There are so many possibilities that lay outside of the norm.

I invite you to ask yourself how you could take more control of your time today.

In order to effectively execute this exercise, we need to make sure we're choosing our higher brains (see Chapter 5). We can take a look at our list to plan and prioritize what truly matters in our lives.

I want to stress that even something that is restful and rejuvenating is still a great choice, even with nothing produced at the end like a clean sink or folded laundry.

You get to decide that it's okay to have laundry in the laundry basket and not put it away. You may decide that you want to spend your time outdoors, not preparing an elaborate, home-cooked meal but instead tossing pasta in water and having spaghetti for dinner. The point is it's up to you. Put your focus on what matters to you.

If you do this consistently, you'll feel like you're creating more time by virtue of simply being more deliberate with your choices. You'll feel as if you have more time in your schedule.

When we feel like we're spread too thin, that's a sign that we're doing too many things at once. In my program, I help my moms focus on achieving one or two goals at a time. We don't tackle everything on the list at once.

If you tighten your focus and give all of your mental, emotional, and physical self to completing those couple of things, you'll actually complete them, and you'll feel momentum and accomplishment. It's such a win-win.

Boss Brain, Employee Mindset

This comes from approaching your life like you're the boss. Imagine you are the CEO of [your name] Life, Inc. A boss decides ahead of time what strategies are the best and how to follow through on those.

You then get to switch over to the employee mindset. Shrug off the pressure from being in charge and focus on following through with what "boss brain" put into motion. There may be distractions that come your way, but the boss has spoken.

The key to feeling you have more time is in the follow-through of what your "boss brain" has decided.

If time feels like a diminishing resource in your life, be aware of your mindset around the construct of time (what are your beliefs about having enough or not having enough time?), choose deliberately how you're going to spend your time, and follow through on your choices.

Time management is a huge part of my daily coaching sessions, from mamas who have new babies and are juggling older siblings, housework, and time to themselves to other mamas who feel like they live in their cars because their children are so busy to other mamas still who work and want to maximize the time they have with their little ones...

I have seen an incredible variety in what the modern mama takes on. If you would like my help organizing your time and maximizing this stage of your motherhood, please click this link, https://www.daniellethienel.com/my-calendar-page, and set up a time to chat.

Chapter 11 Key Takeaways

- Become a Cyclone Mom by moving toward balance, supported by the thought that you have enough time. Experiment by choosing one day where you consciously focus on thinking the thought, "I always have enough time." Notice how you feel and what you get accomplished that day.

- Our mental constructs of time can get in our way. Become more conscious about what time really is. What are your thoughts about time in the thick of a busy day home with kids versus the thoughts you have when you are on vacation? What's different within the same construct of a 24-hour day?

- "Create more time" by virtue of simply being more deliberate with your choices. Do a time audit. Take 2 or 3 days and keep track of how you spend your time. Afterwards, inventory where you have time leaks and make more intentional choices of how to spend your time going forward.

- When we feel like we're spread too thin, that's a sign that we're doing too many things at once. What can you let go of? What feels important but isn't necessarily something that truly matters to get done?

- Pair your "boss brain" with an "employee mindset" for optimal results.

PART 3:

CALM IN THE CENTER OF THE CYCLONE: STEP INTO YOUR POWER

CHAPTER 12:

Three Critical Tools

If God is for me, who can be against me?
~Romans 8:31

I wanted to include a section on just a few of the tools that can help you implement the Cyclone Mom Method into your life.

When I take a step back and look at the big picture, at helping you build a life where you are calm, in control, and confident at any stage in your motherhood, you need both the steps to take and new skills to implement.

There's a quote that's attributed to many famous people that says something along the lines of, "Doing the same thing over and over again and expecting different results is the definition of insanity."

Combining the steps of the Cyclone Mom Method as laid out in Chapters 7-11 and the skills I'll explain in this chapter will bring you closer to becoming a Cyclone Mom who knows how to step into her God-given power.

Below are three of my favorite tools to teach new coaching clients.

B Minus

This is the tool I specifically referred to earlier in the book when discussing perfectionism.

The two-line synopsis of the B Minus tool is to grade your actions and deem a "B minus" grade as good enough in all that you do. If an A+ is prepping an elaborate, home-cooked meal, then allow a B- for boiled spaghetti and sauce from a jar.

I am a recovering perfectionist. I felt like striving for perfection served me well in my previous career as a professional ballet dancer. There was a discipline to upleving my technique and striving for perfection.

But, as soon as I became a mom, perfectionism became a huge hindrance to my peace and satisfaction in life. When I tried to be perfect in this new area of my life, I was overwhelmed. I soon found that my perfectionism was taking me in the opposite direction I wanted. Striving for things to all be going perfectly well sets you up for all things to never go well. Trying to hit that A+ was keeping me from hitting the finish line at all and actually getting things done. So, I was perpetually in striving mode to get things done and never completed anything.

We're after the result of *progress*, not a perfect end result. Making progress may require some mess along the way, but at least you will be in motion, moving forward instead of being stuck.

So, next time you want to throw in the towel, not start a task, or feel paralyzed by trying to be perfect, remind yourself that a B- is good enough.

I have specifically seen a drop in people-pleasing behavior as a result of this tool in my life. Others have found that they are able to make progress in their goals and dreams. The biggest takeaway I offer you is that the B minus tool can be the difference between feeling calm and feeling overwhelmed.

Life on Earth is not designed to be perfect, my mama friend. Leave perfection for heaven. Accept B minus while you're here on this beautiful planet. This tool allows you to have so many wonderful experiences and helps you progress instead of focusing on perfection.

The Model

This tool builds off of the premise we have discussed throughout this book that your thoughts create your feelings.

The Model is the creation of Brooke Castillo, the founder of The Life Coach School. I initially learned this from her, and it is a system I use in my own coaching on a daily basis. It has become my number one tool in my own self-coaching practice as well as the foundational tool in my life coaching business.

It goes like this:

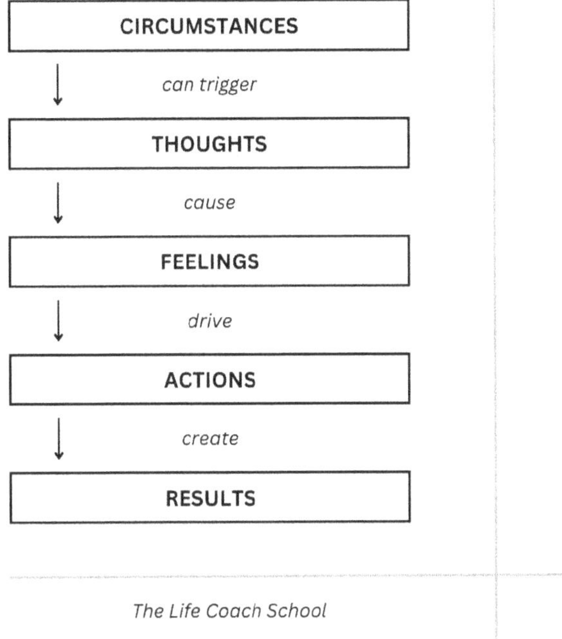

The Life Coach School

In this succinct and orderly, five-lined framework, we can gain control of what is *really* taking place in our lives right now. In this list, we can start at the top and move downward or start at the bottom and move upward.

Most importantly, you can begin to already recognize where thoughts and feelings are in their respective places that you might not have known before.

The Model is, first and foremost, an awareness tool and expands outward to show us where to start as we then embark on the process of creating change. When we understand that a more direct route to the lives we want doesn't start with action, or that our circumstances are not what are the cause of our results, we become capable of affecting the change we want to see.

For example, let's say you are visiting your in-laws, and your mother-in-law says something rude about your appearance.

"Gee, I sure wish you would put a little more effort into how you look. What example does that set for your children?"

Many of my clients would immediately react to this statement with a feeling that they believe was caused by her words, but when we use the model, we can identify that there is a thought that comes before the feeling that we might not be aware of. It wasn't her words that caused the feeling. Her words caused a thought in our minds that then caused a feeling.

Likewise, a client might identify a circumstance like the example above and move straight into an action (snapping back at the mother-in-law) or a result (a strained relationship with the mother-in-law) that has us blaming what the mother-in-law said as the reason for our terrible experience. Both of these answers neglect key steps in The Model.

Your circumstances guide your thoughts. Your thoughts cause your feelings. Your feelings drive your actions. Your actions determine your results.

Remember this order the next time something difficult happens in your life. It will give you a greater capacity to show up with power and calm in your life.

50/50

When I first came across this concept, I really fought it, but it has become one of the biggest lessons I've learned in my life.

The 50/50 principle is that in this big, wonderful life we've been given, in order to live a full, adventurous life while using all of your gifts and achieving your dreams, it will take having 50% positive and 50% negative feelings in this human existence.

Can you see why I instantly rebelled against that definition?

Stick with me here.

We know from Chapter 4 that our thoughts create our feelings. The feeling creates an emotion that is a literal vibration in our bodies.

We know from The Model tool above that these feelings and emotions are not created by our circumstances. They are not created by what other people say, by the weather, by receiving a diagnosis, or by the actions of our children or spouses. We feel certain ways because we have a thought, positive or negative.

The misconception the 50/50 tackles is that we should choose to be happy and positive all of the time.

What this principle tells us is that if we are happy and positive all of the time, then we haven't really tapped into our fullest potential. We are living smaller than God intended us to live.

Now, you can choose to stay in that routine and stick with the safety you feel by avoiding scary things. You don't have to choose to feel uncomfortable.

But, what if there is something else? What if there is something more that you are made for that your heart wants to go after?

Do you remember the story I told about my own journey at the beginning of this book? I was in total overwhelm. I was blaming everything and everyone. I was blaming my boss. I was blaming the hardship of the renovation and the workers and feeling terrible. I had this story in my mind of the drama about how there was so much to do and I was failing at all of it.

Then, I left my job and was home for several months. I filled myself up with some self-care and focused on my prayer time, and everything was amazing. I was working out, visiting friends, and really diving into my faith. I was showing up for my kids in a way I had always wanted to.

But, after a while, I felt a longing in my heart saying, "I think I was made for more…"

During this time of peace, I was living a 90/10 life. 90% positive and 10% negative.

In order to get to where I am right now, where I upleveled my mental capacity and my emotional health, I stepped into having a bigger life that was full of more negative feelings.

I started doing scary things, feeling fear, and being anxious about putting myself online. That was terrifying! I was creating online posts, writing emails, and trying to be okay with a B minus podcast episode, but it got me to where I am now, connecting with you, a mom I have been called to serve.

The other aspect of a 50/50 life I'd like to point out is that sometimes it's good and appropriate to choose a negative emotion.

After the death of a loved one, after a crummy day, or after a hardship, you get to choose how to feel because you can choose your thoughts, right?

From the tray of emotions you can choose from, sometimes it's appropriate to pick up sadness. It's appropriate and expected to feel anger when someone hurts you.

We can choose multiple thoughts as we process our emotions. When complicated circumstances arise, we can choose the thoughts that serve us so we can process the emotions that are appropriate to our situations.

In the next chapter, we're going to build off of this concept of accepting negative emotions as a part of life. I invite you to join me in coaching your brain to redirect your natural reaction of avoiding, resisting, or reacting to negative emotions.

CHAPTER 13

Processing Negative Feelings

*So let us confidently approach the throne of grace
to receive mercy and to find grace for timely help.*
~Hebrews 4:16

One of the most common responses of my coaching clients to learning that your thoughts influence your feelings is to think, "Oh, okay! I just have to think positively!"

When they think a negative thought, they say, "Oh, that's wrong. I have to think positive," because, as I always highlight to them, this is a simple truth that if you feel better, you will do better.

This is true.

But then, we end up using this thinking against ourselves because I'm here to teach you that just thinking positively doesn't work to get the results you want.

In the 50/50 section, we explored how if all you have are the positive side of things, you're actually living a smaller-than-you-were-made-for life. You have so much untapped potential, mama!

When you embrace that it's not a problem to feel negative emotion, there's more that goes on behind the scenes.

Remember the motivational triad? Our survival brain is designed to help us avoid pain, seek pleasure, and conserve energy.

So, when you feel sad or angry, our survival brains kick in and try to lessen the intensity of our negative feelings through an act of avoidance or resistance.

What I want to teach you is that there is a process to regulate negative emotions in a healthy way.

When you grab the candy bar your survival brain offers you, you take yourself in the wrong direction. You create more negative feelings because you feel terrible after eating it. You haven't moved back into a positive direction. You just increased how much negative you have in your life.

Now, remember how we identified that emotions are just vibrations in your body? So, when you feel embarrassed or scared to get up and give a speech, go for it! Those are just vibrations, and on the other side of that fear is accomplishment and pride.

So, how do you actually process a negative feeling without adding more to your negative bucket?

Step one: pause.

Step two: name the feeling.

Step three: describe the feeling in detail.

Step four: question the feeling.

Step five: lean into it and breathe.

Let's explore these steps with another example.

You're stressed about an unexpected bill that came in the mail. Your survival brain says, "Avoid that pain, honey. Go grab yourself some cookies."

On your way to the pantry, you pause.

Then, you ask yourself, "What am I feeling right now? Stressed? Angry?" Name it. At first, there may be many names that fit, but pick the emotion that you deem as the biggest, most problematic emotion of the moment for you. We often have more than one emotion present, but just pick one.

Then, describe the feeling. Where do you feel it in your body? How does it feel? It could be a dropping sensation in your stomach, a shaking in your arms, a sharp feeling in your heart, etc.

Notice that if you are naming and describing the feeling, what are you not doing? You're not in the swirl of, "I'm terrible. I should have known better. This is awful and it's all my fault."

This process helps you get outside of your head for a moment and instead put awareness into your body where you can best process it.

Now, we can clearly question the feeling. Why am I feeling this way? We know that thoughts create feelings, so we can start to work backwards and identify the thoughts that have triggered this vibration in your body.

You lean into this process. Breathe and process. Breathe some more.

This could take you a few minutes or a few days, but it will help you feel better.

Whether you write it out or simply close your eyes and work your way through the steps, this simple system is the key to processing negative emotions without getting hijacked by your lizard brain.

Negative emotions are a part of living a full and happy life. Learning how to regulate those emotions without adding more negativity to your life is a skill that will help you become a calm, confident mom who is in control of the outcomes in her life.

CONCLUSION:

The Discomfort Corridor

I love this quote Brené Brown uses in her writing (which is actually a quote from Teddy Roosevelt).

"It is not the critic who counts; not the man who points out how the strong man stumbles, or where the doer of deeds could have done them better. The credit belongs to the [person] who is actually in the arena, whose face is marred by dust and sweat and blood; who strives valiantly; who errs, who comes short again and again, because there is no effort without error and shortcoming; but who does actually strive to do the deeds; who knows great enthusiasms, the great devotions; who spends himself in a worthy cause; who at the best knows in the end the triumph of high achievement, and who at the worst, if he fails, at least fails while daring greatly."

If you live a 50/50 life, you are daring greatly.

When my mama in coaching feels uncomfortable, I help her not run back and hide and say, "Forget this. I'm not doing this anymore." I help her move through because she is eventually going to get to the promised land.

The number one lesson that will help you dare greatly and live in the arena is to realize that everything you want is on the other side of discomfort.

The path to hitting your goals leads directly along a corridor of uncomfortable feelings.

Remember our GPS analogy? The place you start is where you are right now. The specific goal you've set, that specific destination you've punched in the coordinates and are ready to go?

The path to your dreams is along a corridor of discomfort.

Our brains are wired to keep us away from feeling uncomfortable!

This is why I coach. This is why you can have all of the answers and still need a coach to guide you, to cheer you on, and to get you through the uncomfortable feelings to a larger pile of success.

This journey is going to be tough. It's not easy. Nothing worthwhile ever is.

The person who is willing to feel the most uncomfortable is one with their dreams. Every time. It's important to learn how to process feelings and lean into the discomfort.

I had a client the other day tell me, "Danielle, I was avoiding doing this thing for three months! I felt terrible about what it would be like. Then, I processed that terrible feeling, and it took me all of two minutes to feel a shift. I then finally did it! I had kept myself from getting it done because I was so afraid of what it would feel like, but once I allowed for fear, I was able to just do it!"

If you take away one thing from this book, it is that discomfort is okay. It is safe to feel uncomfortable. It's safe to have negative feelings and vibrate at that frequency sometimes. At the same time, there is a way to move from feeling negative all the time to being the calm, in control, and confident mom God created you to be. Your life of peace, joy, and balance in the midst of a busy life awaits you.

If you want a cheerleader, an encourager, or someone to say, "Keep going! You're almost there!" - I'm here for you. If you want someone who will support you, give you accountability, show up with love (sometimes tough love), and create a judgment-free zone for you to thrive in, I've got your back. If you want someone who can guide your thoughts and teach you new tools and skills to continue upleveling your life, goals, and dreams, then contact me here: https://www.daniellethienel.com/my-calendar-page.

I work with mamas just like you every day, and I help them do incredible things. Things like not yelling at their kids, creating thriving businesses, creating more time in their schedules for what matters most to them, and walking uprightly with peace and power.

Start with the steps in this book. If you want to go further and reach higher, here is your chance: https://www.daniellethienel.com/my-calendar-page.

Until we meet again, peace be with you,

Danielle

Resources

Book a call: https://www.daniellethienel.com/my-calendar-page

Podcast link: https://www.daniellethienel.com/podcasts/the-peaceful-mind-podcast

Website link: https://www.daniellethienel.com/

Blog link: https://www.daniellethienel.com/blog/

Instagram link: https://www.instagram.com/daniellethienelcoaching/

About the Author

Danielle is a wife, mom of three, member of the Catholic faith, certified life coach, and podcast host – and she's familiar with the stress and overwhelm busy moms face on a daily basis. She found herself dreaming of the day she would feel a sense of peace and control... and found the way!

She believes that we have the power to create any result we want for our lives and that this power comes from Christ. Our loving God placed desires for peace, balance, and a better life in our hearts for a purpose, and He gave us our minds to co-create with Him while on Earth.

Danielle's story started when she was working outside the home at a job that didn't align with what she truly wanted. She was in the middle of renovating a house, moving her parents, taking care of kids, driving her kids to all their different extracurricular activities, and not taking care of herself. She thought she could manage everything, but all she really accomplished was managing herself into a sickbed.

She contracted the flu and bronchitis and was forced to be still for two whole weeks. During that time, something she can only describe as "divine" happened. She knew in her soul that she was being divinely guided. She listened to that voice and started making changes in her life that would allow her to be at home, prioritize everything going on, and focus on her faith, family, and herself.

Suddenly, everything started to fall into place. She learned a completely different approach to everything: a process and a blueprint to living life from a place of total control. Life coaching offered a whole new way of doing things in a simpler, sustaining, and empowering way. She became certified as a life coach with The Life Coach School and then studied further, achieving an Advanced Certification in faith-based coaching.

She has since focused her life coaching practice on helping other moms find the joy, balance, and peace she is now an expert in creating. She's dedicated to maximizing her clients' God-given potential and helping moms care for themselves more deeply - mentally, emotionally, and spiritually - so they can have lives filled with more peace, balance, and joy.

Danielle believes that we are all born with a gift we were meant to share. Coaching is the vehicle she was given to share her gift. She can show you how to find your path, too.

Any reader, any mom, is invited to meet Danielle using this link to book a time on her calendar: https://www.daniellethienel.com/my-calendar-page.

Acknowledgments

This book is dedicated to:

Mary, Blessed Mother of God, for her remarkable example, guidance, protection and intercession.

My mom- for always providing all I needed to get to where I am today. I love you so very much.

My twin daughters who first made me a mom. May you be empowered by this book if and when you become a mom one day.

Every mom who reads this book and takes action on its wisdom- know your efforts will greatly impact not only your life and family but will then truly change the world. I applaud you and I am praying for your mom-life journey everyday.

All my own coaches and mentors past and present and each and every one of my own coaching clients whose impact on me is immeasurable- without you this book would not have been possible.

Kim- for being the best teammate to make a deep desire of my heart now exist outside of me and in the world - I know you were an answer to prayer.